Emotion Pictures

Emotion Pictures

THE 'WOMEN'S PICTURE', 1930-55

Hilton Tims

Foreword by Ann Todd

COLUMBUS BOOKS · LONDON

For Anna and Oliver

Copyright © 1987 Hilton Tims

First published in Great Britain in 1987 by
Columbus Books Limited
19-23 Ludgate Hill, London EC4M 7PD

Designed by Marian Morris

British Library Cataloguing in Publication Data

Tims, Hilton
    Emotion pictures: 'the women's picture',
    1930-55.
    1. Moving-pictures—History   2. Women
    in moving-pictures—History
    I. Title
    791.43'09'043   PN1995.9.W6

ISBN 0–86287–326–6

Typeset in Linotron Melior by Falcon Graphic Art Ltd
Wallington, Surrey
Printed and bound by R.J. Acford
Chichester, Sussex

Acknowledgements

FOR THEIR HELP, advice and encouragement I should like to express my thanks to Muriel Box (Lady Gardiner), Bruce Crowther, Laura Marcus, Gill Rowley, June Sampson, Anna Tims, Oliver Tims, Gary West, Carolyn Whitaker and Charles Wilson.

H.T.

About the Author

HILTON TIMS has worked in journalism since 1950, for the BBC, for the London *Daily Mail* (as show-business, theatre and music critic), as a film critic for various publications including the Bristol *Evening World* and the United Newspapers group, and as opera critic for the London *Evening News*. He is currently video columnist for *Options* magazine and assistant editor for the Surrey Comet group of newspapers. He has also had two historical novels published. Married to journalist and author June Sampson, Hilton Tims lives in Kingston upon Thames.

Contents

Foreword

SO MANY MEMORIES are stirred by the titles, names and images in this book, and so many pleasures remembered.

For what woman in those magical years of the cinema – the 'thirties, 'forties and early 'fifties – failed to enjoy the sensations of the vicarious tear or the thrill of a romance?

The appeal of the 'women's picture' as a harmless outlet for emotion was both therapeutic and irresistible for many of us, but, most importantly, I think, it offered enjoyment and a source of escapism at a time when the lives of the majority of women who saw them were hidebound by social convention and economic restraints.

I found myself wondering, as I read Hilton Tims's evocative survey of those movies, minor as well as masterpiece, whether indeed the cinema itself has kept pace with the great advance in the average woman's situation during the past few years.

The 'women's picture' of today is a rarer phenomenon. And, within my own profession, where now are the great roles which once came the way of Bette Davis or Katharine Hepburn or, in the case of *The Seventh Veil* or *The Passionate Friends*, myself? These were roles which audiences lived through with us.

Those characters, and the emotions they generated, left indelible memories. I am continually being reminded, forty years later, of the famous scene in *The Seventh Veil* in which James Mason beat my hands with his cane as I played the piano . . . only a moment, but it has never been forgotten.

A taxi-driver who recognized me after seeing the film recently on television refused to take my fare because, he explained, doing so would destroy his image of the film. Such was the power of the 'emotion picture'.

I am sure everyone, especially every woman, who thrilled to such moments in the great era of the women's picture – and still do whenever they are revived on television – will share the affection and pleasure with which this book recalls its history and times. And I congratulate Hilton Tims on his tribute to these lovely old films.

Ann Todd.

'What Every Woman Wanted to See'

FROM THE START the movies created a new natural element for women. Men made movies and women made up the majority audience for them. The best-remembered caption cliché of the silent cinema was, after all, 'Will ladies kindly remove their hats'!

As unknown actors and actresses began to crystallize into stars it was mainly women admirers who shaped their stardom. Women wrote their fan-mail. Women bought the fan magazines. Their demand for ever more information about the stars' fashions and affairs, scandals and styles was insatiable.

Theda Bara and Pola Negri, those pioneer super-stars, were packaged and sold as man-bait — but it was women's fascination with their clothes and make-up and hairstyles and off-screen exploits which transformed them into icons of glamour unparalleled, to be copied and cloned the world over.

It didn't take long for the early movie moguls to grasp the obvious equation. Women were making movies a seller's market. The next logical step was to make movies specifically for women.

Gloria Swanson drew a shrewd blueprint for the women's picture in her autobiography *Swanson on Swanson*:

Here was what every woman who had ever left a husband wanted to see — how he looked when he first understood that she was gone. Motion pictures allowed her to be a fly on the wall at the most secret moment of her husband's life. No wonder people sat enthralled in darkened theatres all over the world in the presence of those big close-ups. Their effect was indelible. Nothing we had ever had before, in books or plays, written or spoken, could begin to match their impact.

She was writing about a film called *Don't Change Your Husband* made by Cecil B. DeMille in 1918. By then the women's picture had already been established in its cruder form. Theda Bara had erupted into the filmgoer's

Two leading lights of emotion pictures (opposite), Joan Crawford (left) and Constance Bennett; above, Fredric March (left) and Charles Farrell (right); right, Conrad Nagel.

consciousness three years earlier, inventing 'The Vamp'. An unknown Rudolph Valentino had just arrived in Hollywood. Miss Swanson herself was poised to become the empress of the fan and fashion magazines, embodying the hitherto undreamed-of glamour women would crave for.

Through the era of the silent movie the female audience increasingly became a prime marketing target. Male stars like Valentino, Ramon Novarro and John Gilbert commanded phenomenal hero-worship, greater and farther-flung than any man had ever received previously.

Everyone, man and woman alike, clamoured for Garbo movies. Yet they were essentially women's pictures. It was a shrewd tactic on the part of producers who recognized full well where the key to box-office power lay. When couples went to the movies, it was the wife or sweetheart who would determine more often than not which film to see.

The 'talkies' coincided with a period in which women were finding themselves with more disposable income and greater freedom for using their time recreationally. Not yet conditioned or expected to go out to work, they had time to spare between attending to household chores and welcoming the breadwinner home at the end of the working day.

Cinemas were strategically located: in town centres for those who felt like rounding off a spot of shopping with a couple of hours' entertainment (one of the great women's pictures, *Brief Encounter*, even made use of such a ritual as a cornerstone of its drama), or scattered through the suburbs, just round the corner from home.

The programme schedules were convenient, too. You could buy your ticket and take a seat at any time that suited you. The matinée performance was tailor-made for women. And so, with the coming of the talkies and the 'thirties, were the films they could count on seeing.

Ann Harding (opposite, left) and
Ruth Chatterton (opposite, right).

'A Film for the Ladies' was a common catch-line on advertisements of this period.

But a far greater recommendation was the Star. The women's picture had become, and would remain, a star vehicle. Many of the names synonymous with them had successfully navigated the tricky transition from silents to talkies: Garbo (but not John Gilbert, her most popular co-star in the silent days), Joan Crawford, Kay Francis, Norma Shearer, Constance Bennett, Nancy Carroll, Janet Gaynor, Claudette Colbert, Pauline Frederick, Robert Montgomery, Conrad Nagel, Ronald Colman, Herbert Marshall, Charles Farrell, Fredric March.

Ruth Chatterton's stage-trained voice was the making of her as a movie star at a later age than most.

And within the first three years of the new talkies decade three actresses would make their marks on the movies, and women's pictures in particular, which would never be erased — Barbara Stanwyck, Bette Davis and Katharine Hepburn. These stars were more distinctly created for and by women's pictures than for or by any other aspect of their considerable cinematic range.

Yet that very term 'women's picture' has gone down in the language of movies as an expression of, at best, scoffing condenscension and, at worst, ridicule. The words carry a built-in sneer. Break the genre down into its many sub-divisional descriptions — melodrama, weepie or weeper, tear-jerker, sob-story, soap opera or soaper, four-hankie job — and the sneer comes close to contempt.

Unlike the western or the gangster movie or sci-fi or film noir (in all of which the male character is dominant) the women's picture has rated neither serious study nor consideration. More often than not it is looked on sniffily or tolerated indulgently as a barely legitimate off-shoot of mainstream cinema. 'A Film for the Ladies' could be read as a demeaning slogan meaning 'it will please women' (and is therefore best avoided).

Oh, certainly, it has produced the odd classic, but more by chance or whim than by design. It's quite the fashion, after all, to damn even *Gone with the Wind* with faint praise.

Why?

The women's picture, it's true, has seldom aspired to great art even when, by fad or fluke, it has been deemed to attain it. Rather, it's always been a formula geared to entertainment, escapism, wish-fulfilment. But equally, by and large, so was the western.

What has condemned it, more than any other transgression, in the esteem of critics and serious students of the cinema, is its very commercialism. The women's picture has always been the movie equivalent of the romantic novel, the women's-magazine story, the pot-boiler — hardly worthy of consideration!

Moreover — and worse — it deals and dabbles in an area of story-telling that is anathema to purists — emotionalism. That one element, better than any other, defines the women's picture.

In the heyday of the 'thirties and 'forties it aimed for the heart, not the head. The last thing audiences of those decades needed was to be

13

intellectualized or have their thoughts provoked. They wanted escape — from the Depression and the ominous political climate in the 'thirties, from war and its drab aftermath in the 'forties; from the hard, humdrum everyday life the majority of people who went to the cinema led through both decades.

The high, wide, handsome emotionalism of the women's picture was both antidote and tonic. It offered the tempting forbidden fruits of romance and passion, the more illicit the better, at a safe remove. It supplemented the avid public taste for high-life gossip and scandal of those days by showing a glossy life-style legions of women day-dreamed about. At a practical level it established new and glamorous trends in clothes, hairstyles, furnishing decor and social habits (the cocktail, women smoking) which could be copied easily and relatively cheaply.

It wasn't necessary for a women's picture always to be be 'romantic', but it had to be 'emotional'. And the stronger the emotion the better, whether it came packaged as love or hatred, loyalty or deceit, suffering or sacrifice, betrayal or murder.

George Cukor, regarded as the greatest 'women's director' (a description he didn't care for) explained his approach to a scene in Gavin Lambert's book *On Cukor*:

> My first reaction is always emotional. Even when I describe scenes, I describe them emotionally. I don't weep or anything, but there's always some part of me left bloody on the scene I've just directed. That's what gives it intensity.

In comedy or drama Kay Francis (above) was Hollywood's ace scene-stealer. Norma Shearer (opposite) was Hollywood's gracious First Lady of the 'thirties.

14

ace scene-stealer of the age. She could switch from noble heroine (to the extreme of playing Florence Nightingale in *The White Sister*) to arch-bitch with effortless facility. Women flocked to her movies, as much to ogle her wardrobe and legendary elegance as to thrill to her emoting. Off-screen she was consistently voted the best-dressed star in Hollywood.

Ann Harding represented style and class, a glacially blonde forerunner of Grace Kelly and known to the trade as the 'queen of the weepers'. Ruth Chatterton made her mark as the upper-class woman of breeding and an actress of integrity though not, in her roles, above committing the occasional romantic indiscretion.

Constance Bennett, tough and vivacious, had a gritty way of coping with her emotional traumas and, away from the set, was an ace at burnishing her image with the high-flying newsworthiness of her private life. Both she and her equally celebrated actress sister Joan Bennett had eloped as schoolgirls. Constance had married at sixteen as a dare. It lasted two months but at nineteen she was the wife of a millionaire playboy. Later she became the Marquise de la Falaise de la Coudraye by winning Gloria Swanson's French nobleman husband from her and she had a steamy long-term romance with the Latin heart-throb Gilbert Roland.

Then there were Norma Shearer, irreproachably gracious, never less than saintly; Irene Dunne, from much the same mould; Mary Astor, whose screen image of hauteur and latent bitchery would survive the public sen-

The recipe of the archetypal women's picture was fairly inflexible. The principal protagonist had to be a woman. She may be good, she may be bad, but she was always strong, individualistic, dominant; these were the characteristics that forged the greatest of the stars who played them — Greta Garbo, Bette Davis, Joan Crawford, Barbara Stanwyck. They are the ones we remember now.

But in the 'thirties there were others, near-forgotten since, who rivalled them in their fans' esteem.

Dark-haired, mercurial Kay Francis was the

15

sation of a headline-making divorce case; and sweet Loretta Young, whose early off-screen affairs, not least one with Spencer Tracy which threatened to scuttle his contract and career, would have fuelled far more scorching screenplays than those she featured in, if only the censor had allowed.

Strong women all. And their men?

However varying the characters they played, the actors shared certain characteristics in common, most distinctively those qualities associated then with 'the English gentleman'. Many of them had, indeed, come from Britain or the colonies.

Their prototype was Ronald Colman (born in Richmond, Surrey), who had safely negotiated the transition from silents to talkies with his appeal romantically enhanced by the firm but gentle, unaccented and quintessentially English timbres of his voice and diction.

In his wake followed Britons who would become mainstays of the women's picture — Leslie Howard, Claude Rains, Herbert Marshall, Clive Brook, Ian Hunter, Brian Aherne, Cary Grant and George Brent who, born and raised in Ireland when it was still part of Great Britain, had fled to the United States to escape arrest for Republican involvement with the Black and Tans.

The next best thing to a British presence was an American variant. Gary Cooper, Lew Ayres, Robert Montgomery and Fredric March exuded the strong, quiet dependability of the English school.

The Hungarian Paul Lukas and the Frenchman Charles Boyer personified the continental charmer — suave, seductive and maybe slightly caddish — while John Boles and Conrad Nagel served as American facsimiles of their model.

These were the sophisticates. It fell to the all-American regulars, usually more youthful and slightly more callow, to lighten a movie's mood with high spirits or good-natured bonhomie, often in second-lead roles: fresh, uncomplicated guys like Grant Withers, Robert Young, Joel McCrea, Warren William and James Stewart.

In practice, however, it was the rare women's picture in which an actor, however strong his role or equal his star billing, did not play second fiddle to the female star. The whole premise of the genre was to win identification with subject, situation and character from the female audience.

Given those conditions, it says much for Humphrey Bogart that, unknown and buried somewhere near the bottom of the cast-lists, he first began to attract notice in a couple of women's pictures, Bad Sister and Three on a Match, both of which, incidentally, featured an equally obscure Bette Davis.

Indeed, the genre provided rungs on the ladder for many a jobbing actor climbing towards subsequent stardom, including Ray Milland, David Niven, Robert Taylor and the one who would become the most heart-stirring male lead in one of the greatest women's pictures of all, Clark Gable.

Behind the cameras a number of directors who nowadays command cult worship made the women's picture their speciality — George Cukor, Frank Borzage, Edmund Goulding, Vic-

The English gentleman was the
role model for the romantic
leading man of the 'thirties,
personified by Clive Brook (top
left), Herbert Marshall (left) and,
ironically the most English of them
all, the Hungarian-born Leslie
Howard (above).

17

'WHAT EVERY WOMAN WANTED TO SEE'

tor Fleming, Michael Curtiz, Curtis Bernhardt, Douglas Sirk and, often overlooked as a 'women's director', Alfred Hitchcock, who, under a coating of suspense, habitually returned to the form he dominates with *Rebecca*.

With the 'forties and the Second World War the women's picture reached its high-water mark. The mood subtly changed, the tones shifted, but in essence the formula, given contemporary influences, remained the same. Escapism was still the objective and with the

depredations of war was judged to be even more necessary than in the decade before.

New stars emerged but they were extensions of the well-established ones. With the end of the 'thirties several illustrious careers effectively bowed out — those of Ruth Chatterton, Kay Francis, Ann Harding, Norma Shearer, Janet Gaynor and, most sensationally of all, Garbo.

The survival rate among the men was higher, but not in women's pictures. They tended to diversify into tougher areas. But for John Boles, Neil Hamilton, Warren William, Conrad Nagel and Clive Brook the halcyon days were over. Character roles were the best they could settle for.

For some stars, however, the 'forties brought an even greater era. Davis, Crawford and Stanwyck were to scale higher emotional peaks which would make them legends.

The younger generation of stars introduced fresh characteristics, though the guidelines that staked out the characters they portrayed remained largely unchanged.

Greer Garson became the replacement Norma Shearer, on the strength, ironically, of *Mrs Miniver*, which Shearer had rejected (she subsequently admitted it was one of the worst

A Broadway role as one of the most romantic Englishmen, the poet Robert Browning in The Barretts of Wimpole Street, *earned Brian Aherne (left) his Hollywood contract.*

career decisions she ever made). Ingrid Bergman carried over the Scandinavian mystique of Garbo but contrived to stay true to her own distinctive personality.

The dark-haired allure of Kay Francis was picked up by Merle Oberon, while Vivien Leigh and Joan Fontaine each revealed new facets of the thoroughbred qualities of an Ann Harding.

If the new breed of star bore a 'forties stamp which distinguished her from her 'thirties predecessors it was a softening element. Wartime women in movie terms had to be warmer, gentler, more compliant; the reverse of — and perhaps a reaction against — the exigencies of wartime life and conditioning which made women more independent and resilient. The escapist factor still held true in the women's picture.

The customer, so the theory ran, demanded the opposite of the environment she knew in daily life — in the 'thirties, decisive, go-getting heroines, the equal of any man at a time when most women were housebound; in the 'forties, tenderly keeping home fires burning at a time of war which had pitched so many of them out of the kitchen and into the forces or factories.

19

During those years many of the male stars, like Gable, Robert Taylor, Tyrone Power, David Niven and James Stewart, on whom the female audience counted for romance, went to war and put their careers on hold.

It's a feature of films of this period, often overlooked, that the romantic lead surreptitiously became older, even middle-aged, and screenplays frequently adapted themselves accordingly, extolling the ecstasies or heartaches of a spring and autumn relationship (Joan Fontaine and Charles Boyer in *The Constant Nymph*, Greer Garson and Ronald Colman in *Random Harvest*, Bette Davis and Claude Rains in *Mr Skeffington* and *Deception*, Joan Fontaine and Orson Welles in *Jane Eyre*.

The old guard would pick up the threads again after they had pocketed their discharge papers and soldier on into the 'fifties. But they came home to their studios to find new competition firmly entrenched: principally Gregory Peck, Joseph Cotten and Dana Andrews.

Not that the specifics had changed. Peck, Cotten and Andrews, though contrasting in personality, conformed to at least one basic requirement of the Type. They were strong, taciturn and generally sympathetic. With a modification of accent they could even pass muster as English gentlemen, as Peck did in *The Paradine Case*, Cotten in *Love Letters* and Andrews in *Britannia Mews* (though his lines had to be dubbed by an English actor).

It fell to England itself to break the star stereotype of the romantic lead Hollywood imagined women's pictures required. James Mason's sadistic impulses and silkily threaten-

Like Robert Young, Robert Taylor started out as the fresh-faced American college boy type but soon cultivated a more romantic aura.

ing voice struck, first in Britain, later in America, a new, hitherto unpredicted chord of female response.

But by the time he was summoned to Hollywood the women's picture was a fast-fading genre. With the 'fifties television was beginning to take over its function and its market: afternoon soap operas, re-runs of the old tear-jerkers ... The emotion picture hadn't lost its power over women by any means, but its circumstances were changing radically.

Ironically the movie industry counter-attacked with a final salvo of women's pictures in the 'fifties and early 'sixties, lushly packaged in the time-honoured trappings of the form — luxury, high-gloss emotion, fashions to match.

Susan Hayward, unjustly tagged the poor man's Bette Davis, Lana Turner emoting Crawford-style and Jane Wyman radiating Chatterton-like integrity brought to them style and glamour the equal of any of their predecessors. The movies were successful. But they couldn't sustain a declining industry. The mass appeal of the cinema was a thing of the past.

It may be significant that the majority of that final crop were re-makes of some of the classic women's pictures: *Back Street, Imitation of Life, Magnificent Obsession, Madame X*. If nothing else, they demonstrated what game old war-horses those heyday movies had been.

What, if anything is the legacy of the women's picture? Derided as a 'school', dismissed by the arbiters of what passes as art or entertainment in the movies, they were given little chance to escape a received image of pot-boilerism, inconsequential and frivolous.

Not a little of the aphorism that 'the more popular an experience, the more contempt it warrants' hung round them.

Yet the women's picture fought back constantly, consistently. It was never a favourite to win Best Picture awards, though some did, and yet there was seldom a year in which an aspect of at least one did not slip into the nominations.

In the 25 years between 1930 and 1955 there were only seven which failed to produce an Academy Award candidate from the annual output of women's pictures. In all but five of those years they yielded a qualifying performance for a Best Actress award and, of those, no fewer than thirteen were outright winners.

In the peak years of 1944 and 1945 all five annual nominations for Best Actress — including the winner, of course — were performances in women's pictures while earlier, in both 1939 and 1940, four of the five annual nominations, including the winner, for Best Picture were specimens of the genre.

Nor did actors fare too badly in them. It was hardly to be expected, least of all by the star himself, that his subordinate playing to a leading lady in full emotional spate was likely to be the stuff of Oscars. Even so, thirteen actors managed to justify nominations between Clark Gable in *Gone with the Wind* (1939) and James Mason in *A Star Is Born* (1954).

Directors similarly had women's pictures to thank for Academy recognition, notably William Wyler, twice an Oscar recipient (*Mrs Miniver, The Best Years of Our Lives*) and three times nominated (*Wuthering Heights, The Letter, The Heiress*). Even Alfred Hitchcock first

entered the Oscar stakes with one (*Rebecca*).

Bette Davis won for two women's-picture performances (*Dangerous* and *Jezebel*) and was repeatedly nominated for others (*Dark Victory, The Letter, Now, Voyager, Mr Skeffington*). Her rival Joan Crawford received her only Oscar for arguably the most emotive performance of her career (*Mildred Pierce*).

The third great lady of women's pictures, Barbara Stanwyck sadly never made home base, at least not until 1982 when she was given an honorary Academy Award 'for superlative creativity and unique contribution to the art of screen acting'. Thus the industry itself, if not its critics, acknowledged the skills and values represented in the women's picture.

In recent years the techniques that went into those movies, the style and sensitivities with which the best of them were made, have been re-evaluated and their contribution to cinema more clearly recognized. Television has thrown new light on the pictures and their makers. Directors such as Goulding, Borzage and Sirk have belatedly acquired cult following among enthusiasts too young to have any memory of

the lack of interest with which so many of their films were tolerated at the time they were produced. Indeed, there is a risk that they are being taken more seriously now than the people who created them ever intended.

The aim of the women's picture was to entertain, to divert. The themes on which they played endless variations rarely reflected real life. They were more often than not deliberately larger than life.

Most women's pictures slotted into specific categories, governed by prescribed laws of plotting, situation, characterization, mood or individual star personality.

Within each of those categories, be it mother-love or eternal triangle or long-suffering illness or the traumas of war, existed stories, characters, emotional effects ranging from the sublime to the ridiculous.

Over-heated some may be; ludicrous some certainly were. But they were fun.

Gregory Peck, cast in the English gent/romantic mould, in The Paradine Case *(above), with Charles Coburn. Opposite: James Mason, glowering and sadistic.*

23

Barbara Stanwyck.

1

A Monstrous Regiment

THERE HAVE BEEN STRONG WOMEN in the movies since the star system began. Women who knew what they wanted and usually got it (though they might have to pay the price). Vamps in the silents; tough little gold-diggers in the early talkies; through both eras, heroines with their backs to the wall, emotionally or economically, who fought back, displaying resilience and/or fortitude for the encouragement and gratification of their sisters in the audience.

Being fantasy figures they were invariably larger than life and unrepresentative of real life. But as symbolic figureheads they were potent images up there on the screen, offering their fans food for thought and a heady wishful sensation of 'there but for the grace of God . . .'

No matter that, if they transgressed moral or legal proprieties in asserting their strengths and rights, they were required to pay the penalty. They had made a point. The mass of women in the vast filmgoing public could identify with them, secure in the illusion that they would react in just the same way should they ever find themselves in the same situation.

This was an area of life in which the cinema, particularly the Hollywood cinema, was way ahead of its time. It produced a breed of female character and actress which only in recent years has begun to be replicated in real life.

It is significant that the three actresses who dominated women's pictures after the arrival of the talkies, Barbara Stanwyck, Bette Davis and Joan Crawford, are best remembered in movie mythology for this type of role.

In the case of each of them the ruthless,

amoral, stop-at-nothing characters they portrayed form only a fraction of their wide-ranging gallery of roles. But it is the hard-boiled character which has immortalized them.

Barbara Stanwyck, who once said 'I've had to push every gate that ever opened to me', is the high-priestess of the tribe.

In the 'eighties — and in her eighties — she was still coming on strong for television in *The Thorn Birds* and *The Colbys* more than half a century after achieving stardom in Frank Capra's 1930 film *Ladies of Leisure*.

Her follow-up role in *Illicit* (1931) established her as a specialist in characters who didn't conform to prevailing climates of taste or morals, women who held out vehemently for independence.

Daring for its time (the notorious Production Code laid down by the Hays Office in response to mounting public outrage at Hollywood's moral laxity on and off the screen was not introduced until 1934), the movie depicted a heroine who unashamedly contends that marriage stifles love and prefers to have an 'illicit' relationship.

Through a succession of 'bad girl' roles, Stanwyck honed the free-spirited edge of her screen personality until it hallmarked her stage image whether in romances, crime dramas, tear-jerkers (the superb *Stella Dallas*), westerns or comedies at which she was wise-crackingly expert.

By the 1940s she had become the undisputed 'strong' woman of the screen. Davis and Crawford may have run her close but Stanwyck had

Tough but sensitive throughout the 'thirties, Barbara Stanwyck cast scruples aside in the 'forties for a series of stop-at-nothing heroines.

25

a head-start over them and hung on to it. Neither of her rivals could approach quite the intensity or ruthless single-mindedness of a Stanwyck character at its most implacable.

The strongest of them tended to be cast in *film noir* thrillers, technically not women's pictures but given a powerful thrust in their direction and an infallible interest for female audiences by her presence in them.

Trace *Double Indemnity* (1944), one of the great *films noir* and probably her most compelling performance, back to its origins in James M.

Barbara Stanwyck in Double Indemnity (above) with Fred MacMurray and in The Strange Love of Martha Ivers (opposite) with Kirk Douglas (seated) and Van Heflin (also in portrait above).

26

Cain's short novel and you find not so much a thriller as a frightening character study of a callous, calculating woman.

Phyllis Dietrichson is Barbara Stanwyck's most memorable role and it is one of Hollywood's inexplicable mysteries that she failed to win an Academy Award for it (Ingrid Bergman got it that year for *Gaslight*).

With brassy sex appeal and iron nerve she ensnares Fred MacMurray's weak insurance agent in a fiendishly clever plot to murder her husband with an implicit promise of sharing the insurance pay-out and herself with him. She has no intention of honouring either commitment.

The character has no redeeming feature save a superficial (and phony) charm and fatal sexual allure. Stanwyck's performance smoulders, the more so because of the cool, matter-of-fact detachment with which she carries the scheme through, pretending a poisonous passion for her chosen accomplice as a cover for dispassionately manipulating him. This is a woman who is ruthlessly selfish and with the cunning not to show it.

For all her history of playing 'no better than she should be' women, Stanwyck had reservations about taking on, in her own words, 'an out-and-out killer'. When she voiced them to director William Wyler he responded with a challenge she, being the mettlesome star she was, couldn't resist: 'Are you a mouse or an actress?'

The performance that resulted set her already distinguished career on a new, even starrier course. Audiences were mesmerized by this

27

Barbara Stanwyck's gullible victim in The File on Thelma Jordon *was Wendell Corey, playing an unhappily married attorney seduced into abetting a murder.*

study in evil and Stanwyck proceeded to give them more.

In *The Strange Love of Martha Ivers* (1946) she was even more villainous.

Curiously overlooked, this long, unwieldy movie is monumental melodrama, an example again of murder packaged with the trimmings of strong female emotionalism.

A prologue sets the tone and introduces the three main characters. Martha Ivers, a young girl living with an overbearing aunt, murders her in an explosion of fury when her plans to run away with Sam, a casual boyfriend, go awry. Another youth, the weak-charactered Walter, witnesses the killing and helps her to cover up her part in it.

The story then jumps eighteen years. Martha has inherited her aunt's fortune and has married Walter to buy his silence. Now a force to be reckoned with in the small-town community, she despises her alcoholic husband — who is running for public office — but is powerless to rid herself of him.

Sam comes back into her life after years of absence and Martha calculatingly draws him into an affair with the intention of persuading him to dispose of Walter. She has always believed he too was present the night she killed her aunt.

But he wasn't and when Martha realizes she has needlessly revealed her guilt to him her true viciousness is unleashed. In a compelling showdown of deceit and counter-deception she gets her due desserts.

Dressed, as it were, to kill, in high 'forties style, Stanwyck's Martha Ivers surpasses even Phyllis Dietrichson in premeditated malevolence, controlling the men in her life and bending them to her will.

The plot, rendered down, is absurdly

novelettish but *The Strange Love of Martha Ivers* is a rare example of all the production elements meshing to elevate unlikely material to quality story-telling — an intelligent script, fine direction and musical scoring, highly combustible star performances.

Kirk Douglas made his screen début and a lasting impression as the dipsomaniac Walter, the first and only weak character he was ever to play. Van Heflin was Sam. He was one of the few actors who could confront and complement Stanwyck on equal terms and their scenes together are riveting clashes of highly charged emotionalism.

A more subdued though no less lethal Stanwyck returned four years later in *The File on Thelma Jordon* (1950), again ensnaring a marked-out male victim for murky reasons of her own, again murdering a wealthy aunt.

Thelma Jordon has the same deceit and ruthlessness as Phyllis Dietrichson and Martha Ivers but also a quality in which both had been conspicuously lacking — vulnerability. She is being manipulated herself by a worthless man from her past.

As cover for his plan to kill the aunt (Thelma herself has to do the deed while he stays safely in the background), she is primed to draw a gullible, unhappily married lawyer (Wendell Corey) into an affair. He is amenably set up to accept her story that she thought she was firing at a night intruder when she cold-bloodedly shoots the old woman.

He helps her to conceal damning evidence and when she is indicted for murder is duped into taking on the prosecution's case and deliberately losing it.

Duly acquitted, she dumps him. But at this point Thelma veers away from the self-serving course steered by Phyllis/Martha. She realizes she has fallen in love with her victim.

Stanwyck toys with the audience's sympathies as teasingly as she does with the lawyer's. Thelma Jordon seems sincere enough, then a look, a hardening expression, a premeditated lie hints at deceit and plants a doubt.

In all three roles Barbara Stanwyck showed herself to be peerless at invoking the psychological extremes of a woman's power over men. And indeed she never undertook any role, be it comic or straightforwardly romantic, in which she allowed herself to yield the upper hand in

The full force of Bette Davis's vindictiveness in The Little Foxes *was reserved for her ailing husband Herbert Marshall and their daughter Teresa Wright.*

character, even if she kept it gloved in velvet.

Bette Davis's excursions into evil were of a more direct thrust. More often than not her badness was qualified, might even be excused, by circumstances or the necessity of taking a position of strength because of the weakness of the men involved.

Unlike Stanwyck's Phyllis Dietrichson or Martha Ivers, a Davis bad-hat was unlikely to be 'rotten to the core' or beyond redemption. When Stanwyck's *Illicit* was re-made a scant two years later with Davis, the character was considerably softened.

'It was junk,' Bette Davis remembered years later. Nevertheless it did the trick for her as it had for Stanwyck and launched her as a star.

She first showed her mettle as a bad lot in *Of Human Bondage* (1934) and it was a revelation. She had pleaded for the chance to play the cheap, vicious Cockney waitress, Mildred Rogers, who blights the life of a medical student obsessed with her (Leslie Howard) in Somerset Maugham's novel. 'An evil heroine such as Mildred was really unheard of in that day,' she recalled afterwards.

The film's most famous scene, in which Mildred, finally rejected by the student, rounds on him with a torrent of pent-up spite, still has the power to shock . . .

I never cared for you, not once. I was always making a fool of you. You bored me stiff. I hated you. It made me sick when I had to let you kiss me. I only did it because you begged me. You hounded me, you drove me crazy and, after you kissed me, I always used to wipe my mouth. Wipe my mouth . . .

The staccato stab wounds of that speech were the blueprint for many a Davis scene to come, a trademark of the venom the world would learn to love.

Life magazine noted that she gave 'probably the best performance ever recorded on the screen by a US actress'.

It was another such scene, wordless this time, which stamps *The Little Foxes* (1941) with a memory of overwhelming callousness.

The screen version of Lillian Hellman's play does not fit conventionally into the women's picture genre, but like so many of Barbara Stanwyck's subjects it is strongly biased towards a female identification by the presence in it of Davis and her dominance over the male characters and the movie.

Interpretation of the iron-willed Regina Giddens led to some discord between Davis and director William Wyler, who wanted to soften the character for the screen. Davis disagreed and got her way.

Years later she would write:

It was the only time in my career I walked out on a film after the shooting had begun. I was a nervous wreck due to the fact that my favourite and most admired director was fighting me every inch of the way as regards my interpretation of Regina.

Thirty years later she was still lamenting that Wyler never again used her.

But she vindicated herself in a performance which was acclaimed, Oscar-nominated and described by the *New York Times* as 'one of the most cruelly realistic character studies yet shown on the screen'.

The *Little Foxes* is a study of a small-town Southern family corrupted by greed. Regina, married to a man (Herbert Marshall) whose kindliness and ineffectuality she despises, wants him to put up the money for a business deal she and her equally grasping brothers are plotting. When he refuses to co-operate, guessing the deal is shady, she turns on him with a fury which brings on one of his periodic heart attacks.

Piteously he begs her to fetch the medication which relieves the pain and pitilessly she makes no move, sensing the attack will be fatal.

The sight of Davis soundlessly watching his death throes, at first struggling to suppress the instinct to help him, then waiting tensely for his life to ebb away, is monstrously chilling in its inhumanity.

A year later Bette Davis was delivering one of her most wildly excessive performances as the worthless sister of Olivia de Havilland in *In This Our Life* (1942).

Based on a Pulitzer Prize-winning novel by the distinguished writer Ellen Glasgow, it was John Huston's second assignment as a director after his success with *The Maltese Falcon*.

The script, potboiled down to emotional basics from a 'literary' source, did little justice to book or author. Nor did it greatly enhance the reputations of its director and star. Nowadays it is best remembered, if remembered at all, for a couple of ephemeral footnotes in Hollywood history books.

It was the first movie to portray a black character as educated and articulate rather than comic, musical or simple-minded. And, uniquely, both its leading ladies were blessed with boys' names. Bette Davis was called Stanley, Olivia de Havilland was Roy!

Here again was a Southern family riddled with neurosis, envy and decay. Roy is the good sister, Stanley the bad one, spoiled, wilful and devoid of scruple.

Davis, who admired the book and its author,

had banked on being the goody-goody girl this time but the studio decided otherwise. So she flounces through the movie in ghastly frocks and unattractive hair-style, wallowing in its emotional quagmire as though hell-bent on getting even with the casting director by giving her all, over the top and then some.

Stanley jilts her own lawyer fiancé (George Brent) in order to steal the decent but too quiescent man sister Roy has married. They run away together and she quickly drives him to suicide with a quintessential Davis tongue-lashing ('I hate you. I hate the day I married you. I hate everything about you . . .').

Meanwhile her cast-off lawyer has found consolation with Roy, whose sisterly forebear-ance begins to seem suspiciously like maso-chism. This development is guaranteed to inflame Stanley's chronic covetousness. She wants him back but he gives her the brush-off during a clandestine assignation.

Furious, she drives off and kills a child in a hit-and-run accident. The car is traced and she contrives to pin the blame on the son of the family's cook, a young black law student whom she accuses of taking her car without permis-sion for a joy-ride. It is her ex-fiancé who uncovers the truth.

Unable to face the consequences, she runs to her wealthy old uncle (Charles Coburn), who has just learned he is dying from an incurable disease. She begs him for money to enable her

Bette Davis gave one of her most over-the-top performances in In This Our Life with Olivia de Havilland (opposite).

In A Stolen Life (right and below) she was good and bad in equal measures as twin sisters both in love with Glenn Ford.

Austrian actress Elisabeth Bergner had set the example for Bette Davis's double exposure in an earlier British version of A Stolen Life.

to flee the country. 'You're not going to need it. You're going to die,' she rants, ever true to form.

This scene is a collector's item. Davis never surpassed it for sheer histrionic delirium. Realizing the old man harbours incestuous designs on her she again jumps into her car and drives off, this time to a providential skid and death.

The valedictory notice on *In This Our Life* has been given succinctly by Bette Davis herself: 'A real story had been turned into a phony film.'

When she was good in *A Stolen Life* (1946) she was very, very good and when she was bad she was horrid. A 'sisters' story again but with a difference: Davis played twins.

The material had provided a popular showcase for the beautiful Austrian actress Elisabeth Bergner in a British production eight years earlier. There were to be some subtle stylistic changes in the Davis version which helped to make it that rarity among remakes, an improvement on the original.

Played out against the rugged mist-shrouded coastline of Maine (it had been Brittany in the earlier movie), the story turns on the love of twin sisters, identical in every feature except nature, for Bill, a lighthouse keeper (Glenn Ford).

Kate, the good one, finds him first only to have him snatched away by Patricia, the one who always gets what she wants. Being an artist and therefore sensitive, Kate yields nobly and finds consolation with an anarchic fellow artist (Dane Clark) who, after several reels, disappears without trace or explanation from the story-line.

Patricia and Bill have married and Kate returns to the old family homestead for a visit. The sisters go sailing. A storm blows up, the boat capsizes and Patricia is swept overboard. Kate desperately tries to save her by clasping her hand but it slips away, leaving the wedding ring in Kate's clenched fist.

She slips it on her own finger for safe keeping and passes out. When she is brought ashore unconscious everybody assumes she is Patricia and Kate has perished.

Thinks: Bill won't know the difference.

But she is soon disabused. Patricia, she learns, was a faithless wife and the marriage was heading for the rocks. She walks out of Bill's life, thereby confirming his suspicion that she must be Kate, his true love, after all ... Patricia wouldn't have been capable of such a sacrificial act.

A Stolen Life demonstrates how the soapiest opera can be kneaded and glossed into an illusion of superior melodrama. Its slender plot is stretched to nearly two hours yet it never

'A midnight girl in a nine o'clock town' . . . and the bell tolled for Bette Davis's career at Warner Bros. with Beyond the Forest, *in which Joseph Cotten was her co-star (below).*

palls. The script by Catherine Turney, who had written the previous year's hit *Mildred Pierce*, had an edge of lively intelligence and sophistication. Curtis Bernhardt's direction was full of pleasing style points and surprises, not least in the trick shots worked out for Davis's dual scenes. Max Steiner provided another admirable musical score.

It was an altogether more adroit movie than its British predecessor, in some degree due, ironically, to the requirements of the Production Code.

In the Elisabeth Bergner version the surviving sister enters into a wholehearted marital alliance with her unsuspecting brother-in-law. Such a flagrant sexual allusion was impossible under Hollywood's censorship rules so the Davis script twists and turns in convolutions of

propriety to make sure Kate and Bill don't stray into any compromising clinches or situations. This has a bonus effect of making Kate's masquerade as the imposter wife more plausible.

Davis's dual characterization, too, was subtler than Bergner's; the differences between the twins — hair-styles, make-up, clothing — which the British film had found necessary to mark were less pronounced and so less artificial.

Critics were, inevitably perhaps, dismissive of what the *Washington Daily News* dubbed 'enough high-powered mush to send millions of impressionable females purring happily over their after-matinée tea'.

In the event, impressionable females purred in their millions to guarantee the film made a fortune.

Bette Davis had one more bad hat to don under her Warner contract, and it nearly destroyed her career.

Beyond the Forest (1949) has become a token title for bad film art — so bad, in the view of some, that its awfulness is an entertainment in itself.

The poster blurbs said it all. 'She's a midnight girl in a nine o'clock town' . . . 'Nobody's as good as Bette Davis when she's bad'.

Gaudy artwork showed Davis spilling out of her blouse, laid back in abandonment, hands behind her head and a cigarette dangling from her mouth. For a Bette Davis movie it was sacrilege.

She was, in fact, past her fortieth birthday when she was contractually obliged to play the 'midnight girl' Rosa Moline, a Madame Bovary of the Mid-West. Indeed she tried to use the age anachronism as a weapon in her bid to duck out of taking on the role but to no avail.

Rosa, married to a kindly but weak small-town doctor (Joseph Cotten), is bored, spiteful and restless for the excitements of Chicago, the nearest centre of civilization (she yearns to wear Dior's New Look).

She strikes up a torrid affair with a Chicago millionaire (David Brian) who keeps a shooting lodge nearby, but he regards her as a sideline.

An elderly rustic chances on one of her bouts of passion in the woods and, knowing her to be pregnant, proposes to inform her husband. She shoots him.

Melodramatics are intensified by a botched abortion resulting in peritonitis. Delirious but more determined than ever to get to Chicago, she makes one final symbolic bid to catch the nine o'clock train but dies alongside the tracks as it pulls out.

The movie can be said to share one quality with the Stuart Engstrand novel from which it was adapted; it's compulsive but for totally different reasons. Lurid, over-excitable and straining credulity, it makes a mockery of the original story's powerfully expressed study of a woman self-destructed by the demons in her own nature.

Edward Albee gave *Beyond the Forest* minor immortality in his play *Who's Afraid of Virginia Woolf?* The shrewish wife Martha who, had she been invented earlier, might have provided a role model for Bette Davis, makes her first entrance with the line 'What a dump!' It signals an argument with her husband over which movie Davis had used it in. The movie was *Beyond the Forest*.

In an interview Joan Crawford, touching on Women's Lib, once said half-jokingly:

> To them I should be some sort of heroine. I brought more men to their knees or actually ruined them than any other actress in Hollywood history. They should order their membership to see old Joan Crawford movies; if anyone could handle those mean male bastards, Joan could.

She exaggerated slightly. Over her 43-year and 80-film career it was Joan Crawford who was more often brought to *her* knees by some mean male bastard turning out to be not quite so mean in her eyes after all.

Crawford's image was always positive. Not until the afternoon of her career did it take on the dominant and indomitable characteristic that posterity accepts as her personal cliché.

She first tried it for size in *A Woman's Face* (1941), her 52nd movie. It was a turning-point, bringing to an end the hugely popular devil-may-care roles she had played in countless comedies and romances and revealing her as a strongly dramatic actress.

It required courage, too. For the first time a Hollywood goddess allowed her features to be disfigured (though MGM wouldn't allow publicity photographs to show it).

A Woman's Face was a straight lift of a Swedish film made three years previously which had starred an Ingrid Bergman still unknown to Hollywood.

Anna Holm, her face hideously scarred in a childhood accident, is the embittered leader of a blackmailing gang. She becomes the mistress of a sinister aristocrat (Conrad Veidt) who intends using her in a plot to murder his young nephew and clear away the only obstacle between him and a fortune.

She meets a plastic surgeon (Melvyn Douglas) who believes he can correct her disfigurement and persuades her to undergo risky surgery.

The operation is a success. Anna emerges a strikingly beautiful woman and her lover arranges a position for her with his nephew's family. However, her new look has brought about a new personality and outlook on life. She becomes attached to the boy whose life she is endangering and in a tense climax she saves his life by shooting the uncle-lover she now despises. The drama unfolds within the framework of her trial and suspense is sustained to the end by the uncertainty of its outcome.

The forceful Crawford style was set in aspic four years later with *Mildred Pierce* and *Humoresque* (dealt with in Chapters 2 and 5), portraying women determined to get what they wanted and letting nothing stand in their way.

By now she had adopted the much-parodied mannish appearance and aggressiveness, augmenting her star image of quasi-masculine strength and authority to be exposed so ruthlessly by her adopted daughter Christine in the book *Mommie Dearest*. However, the broad padded shoulders which became her trademark were not a premeditated accessory to this

image-building. Her clothes were cut that way to counteract the effect of unusually wide-spaced collar bones.

Crawford's first outright 'bitch' role came with *Harriet Craig* (1950), a screenplay which uncannily mirrored her own, at that time unsuspected, domestic regime.

As Christina was to reveal in *Mommie Dearest*, her mother was obsessively house-proud. So was Harriet Craig, a shrew who subordinates everything, most of all her husband (Wendell Corey), to the pathological rigours of her housekeeping. Her selfishness and deep-rooted hatred of men is traced back to childhood and a feckless father who deserted his family.

Harriet is an unmitigated monster. When her husband, whom she superficially affects to care for, is offered promotion which will disrupt her housewifely routine, she spins a tale to his boss which ruins his chances.

She breaks up her young cousin's budding romance and her husband's oldest male friendship. In the end he walks out, taking care

*Gene Tierney concealed her
murderous impulses behind a
mask of calm beauty as the jealous
wife in* Leave Her to Heaven
(opposite).

to smash her favourite vase as a final, though belated, gesture of defiance.

Even so, the movie could be said to have a happy ending of sorts. Alone and rejected she may be but at least Harriet is left with the love of her life — her house.

Crawford's films around this time were beginning to signal the downward slope from which she would salvage only one more worthwhile subject, *Whatever Happened to Baby Jane?*, teaming her for the first and only time with her arch rival Bette Davis.

But she still had one last trump to play in *Queen Bee* (1955).

'I had a chance to play the total bitch . . . I ended up hating myself, honestly feeling that in my death scene I was getting precisely what I deserved,' she told an interviewer.

The role seemed a synthesis of every hard, unscrupulous, domineering woman Hollywood had ever pitted against a weak male will.

Eva Phillips is evil to her very soul, totally selfish and motivated by a compulsion to dominate everyone she can use to further her own ends. Like so many of her prototypes in fiction and movies she is a southern lady, the chatelaine of a Georgia mansion and married to wealthy Avery (Barry Sullivan), whose hatred for her has driven him to drink.

She wrecks her sister-in-law's engagement to the estate manager (John Ireland), once her lover and still, in her twisted reasoning, her 'property'. By pressuring him into renewing the old affair she drives the girl to suicide.

Avery meanwhile is showing a dangerous interest in Eva's young cousin who is visiting them. Eva's malevolence knows no bounds. The manager, aware of her plans for them, sees a way of avenging his fiancée's death. He takes her out for a drive and deliberately crashes the car, killing them both.

'Miss Crawford plays her role with such silky villainy that we long to see her dispatched,' said the *New York Herald Tribune* critic.

Queen Bee is only average melodrama but it makes intriguing viewing nowadays for the way it distils the Joan Crawford image that has passed into posterity — powerful, masculine-strong, intransigent, fabulously costumed.

'Few actresses can resist playing bitchy women,' Gene Tierney wrote in her autobiography. The chance came for her only once but she seized it greedily.

Ellen, in *Leave Her to Heaven* (1945), is perhaps the most chillingly cold and calculating woman Hollywood has ever offered. Tierney, more of a decorative than a dramatic asset to her movies, was nominated for an Oscar. That was a peak year when all the nominations for Best Actress were for performances in women's pictures. The award went to Joan Crawford for *Mildred Pierce*.

Obsessive jealousy was the motif of the story, based on a best-seller by Ben Ames Williams. Ellen has known real love for only one person, her dead father, when she marries Richard Harland (Cornel Wilde) who resembles him. She won't tolerate any divergence of attention or affection from herself.

When his crippled younger brother comes to visit and Ellen perceives the fondness between them she suggests the boy accompanies her for

39

a swim in the lake. She rows far out and in a sequence of accumulating horror, the equal of the death scene in *The Little Foxes*, watches impassively as he is seized by cramp and slowly drowns.

Finding herself pregnant, she can't endure the thought of sharing Richard's love with a child and deliberately throws herself down the staircase to procure a miscarriage.

Her adopted sister Ruth (Jeanne Crain) is their next house-guest. Richard, beginning to have his doubts about Ellen, shows an interest in her. Miscalculating for once, Ellen believes she can win him back by confessing her crimes and repenting. But even as she tells him, she is plotting to poison Ruth.

Richard, repelled, announces he is leaving her. She takes the poison herself after planting evidence that will lead to Richard and Ruth being accused of murdering her.

Leave Her to Heaven studiedly flouted the rules of the genre. John M. Stahl, who had directed such great women's pictures as *Magnificent Obsession* and *Imitation of Life*, shot it in stunning Technicolor and made maximum use of beautiful open-air locations to counterpoint the dark psychological evil at its core.

The stereotype of the Ellen character was given fresh colouring, too, by an outward veneer of quiet charm and refinement, her callousness heightened by the impassive, almost inscrutable surface expression.

A similar kind of charm, reinforced by her customary self-effacement, was exploited for Joan Fontaine's two forays into self-serving evil. She was not altogether at home with it.

Ivy (1947) is an Englishwoman at the turn of the century obsessed with marrying into money, a prospect frustrated by the inconvenience of already being married to a man without it.

Setting her sights on wealthy middle-aged Herbert Marshall, she dispatches both her husband and her clandestine lover by slipping them poison.

Miss Fontaine could affect slyness and deceit

Innocence was Joan Fontaine's regulation image but she could manipulate it shrewdly to whatever ends a role demanded, whether as the poisonous heroine of Ivy *(opposite) or, in* Rebecca, *as the second wife haunted by the ghost of the first, at the mercy of the malevolent Mrs Danvers, Judith Anderson (below).*

plausibly enough but outright wickedness seemed alien to her. *Ivy* was contrived.

More interesting were the off-screen melodramatics which had led to her playing the part. It had first been assigned to her sister Olivia de Havilland. The feud between them which provided Hollywood gossip-writers with such titillating copy was then in full spate

and de Havilland, who had just played a bad lot in *The Dark Mirror* and hated the experience, turned it down. It was then offered to Fontaine who, according to gossip, grabbed it gleefully.

Olivia had the last laugh. She had sensed from the start that *Ivy* would be a commercial failure and so it proved.

Three years later Fontaine tried again in the unequivocally-titled *Born to be Bad* (1950), an early exercise by the now-revered director Nicholas Ray, whose forte was the darker side of human emotions. One wag best summed up the character she played as 'a cross between Lucrezia Borgia and Peg o' My Heart'.

Behind the usual Fontaine façade of wide-eyed innocence, Christabel Craine is, like Ivy, a woman on the make, unprincipled in her pursuit of money, this time among the denizens of San Francisco's publishing and arty circles.

Having lured millionaire Zachary Scott into marriage, she is still not content and makes a pitch for novelist Robert Ryan.

It was routine pulp-fiction but director Ray's skills gave it a certain stylishness which in recent years has converted it, not altogether deservedly, into a cult movie.

The role Olivia de Havilland had detested so much was only fifty per cent of her contribution to *The Dark Mirror* (1946). She played identical twins. Inevitably, one was good, the other bad, but the challenges of interpretation were even more demanding than those Bette Davis faced the same year in *A Stolen Life*.

The impact of this psychological thriller-drama which opens with one of the sisters murdering her lover hinges on the inseparability of the twins visually and in superficial personality.

To heighten and prolong the suspense, the innocent one — whichever she is — loyally

Evil or maligned? Olivia de Havilland dispenses herbal tea – and maybe death – for Richard Burton and Audrey Dalton in My Cousin Rachel *(opposite).*

protects the guilty one. It falls to a psychiatrist (Lew Ayres) who specializes in the psychology of twins to expose the culprit through a series of tests. In the process he falls in love with one (or both?) of them, taking a chance that he has picked the right one.

It wasn't a happy experience for de Havilland. Reluctant to tarnish her image with evil, though realizing that the good half of the dual role compensated, she was constantly in conflict with the director Robert Siodmak.

He persisted, rightly, in pushing her to the limits of expression for the climactic scenes in which the guilty sister is tricked into revealing herself and her latent insanity. 'That horrible Terry . . . haunts me to this day,' she has said in recent times.

De Havilland was at the peak of her powers during this period. She had gone straight into *The Dark Mirror* from *To Each His Own,* for which she won her first Oscar, followed it with *The Snake Pit,* for which she was nominated, and the year after that gained her second Academy Award for *The Heiress* (1949), the most striking and memorable of all her performances.

The role of Catherine Sloper is unique in that it charts with a perfect aesthetic rationale the transformation of a meek, vulnerable woman into a strong, pitiless one through her thwarted love for a worthless man.

The film is set in the nineteenth century in New York's fashionable Washington Square (the title of Henry James' original novel), where Catherine lives with a domineering father (Ralph Richardson) who has little love for her.

A young suitor, Maurice Townsend (Montgomery Clift), pays court to her, knowing she will one day come into a fortune, but her father forbids marriage, recognizing him as a fortune-hunter.

The first offer of love Catherine has ever known gives her the strength to defy parental authority. Her father threatens to disinherit her if she persists in her plans to marry Maurice so she makes plan to elope.

Maurice, informed that she will be cut off without a penny, fails to keep their assignation. As Catherine waits through the night in the silent house, slowly facing up to the fact that he has abandoned her, her heart hardens.

Years later, learning that the father is dead and Catherine is mistress of her own fortune, Maurice returns. At first she receives him coolly, then seems to recapture something of her old feeling for him as he works his charm on her.

Once again he proposes marriage. Once again she accepts, playfully suggesting they elope as they had planned long ago.

That evening at the appointed hour Maurice is at the door. She comes in answer to his knock — and slams the bolts in his face. As he hammers at the door, she climbs the staircase into her destiny of old maidhood. She had liberated herself from the tyranny of men, but at great cost.

'Can you be so cruel?' her aunt-companion asks when she has revealed her intention. Catherine replies with the film's celebrated line: 'Yes, I can be very cruel. I have been taught by masters.'

In the title roles of My Cousin Rachel *and* The Heiress *Olivia de Havilland showed herself expert at disguising an iron resolve with outward charm and reticence.*

The Heiress is superlative film-making, directed with acute perception and attention to detail by William Wyler, superbly acted and, in Olivia de Havilland's characterization, preserving one of the cinema's finest performances.

She followed it three years later with one of the screen's most enigmatic heroines. Was the heroine of *My Cousin Rachel* (1953) good or evil?

Daphne du Maurier's teasing, gripping but ultimately unsatisfactory mystery left the audience to decide. There was no question, however, about de Havilland's deft achievement in raising the question-marks.

She had not been the first choice for the role. Diplomatic feelers had been put out to lure Greta Garbo back to the screen to portray a character which might have seemed tailor-made for her. She declined, as she did tentative offers of the next film de Havilland was to make, *That Lady*.

Rachel is a mystery woman. Philip Ashley, a headstrong young Cornish landowner, played by Richard Burton in his Hollywood début, learns that his cousin Ambrose, who had reared him and to whom he is devoted, has unexpectedly married her during a visit to Italy. But Ambrose's increasingly incoherent letters home begin to suggest that he is being methodically poisoned ('Rachel, my torment'!).

He dies and Rachel arrives on Philip's doorstep. Prepared to denounce her, he is instead overwhelmed by her charm and beauty. Soon, wildly in love as Ambrose had been, he proposes marriage, which she gently rejects.

The arrival of a sinister Italian lawyer throws him into confusion and suspicion that he is a past lover of Rachel's. He becomes dangerously ill after drinking a herbal tea she has prepared and she nurses him devotedly back to health.

But she has now become *his* torment. Convinced that she murdered Ambrose and plans a similar fate for him to gain possession of the estate, he deliberately allows her to fall to her death from an unsafe bridge in the grounds. But the posthumous discovery of another of her letters casts doubts on her guilt. Rachel will be his torment ever more.

De Havilland's performance, full of fascinating details, lulling an audience into sympathy only to arouse suspicion with a look or quiet inflection in her voice, gave the film a distinction it would have otherwise lacked.

It was another Daphne du Maurier novel which inspired perhaps the screen's most abiding study of the power a woman can exert, albeit from beyond the grave.

Of all Alfred Hitchcock's films *Rebecca* (1940) reveals his skill with an essentially emotional subject. Thriller, Gothic mystery . . . whatever label is pinned on it, *Rebecca* will always endure as the perfect women's picture.

One of the first actresses to be considered for the role of the second Mrs de Winter was Olivia de Havilland. It went, of course, to her sister.

Joan Fontaine's success in it is part of screen legend; such a perfection of casting that, seen now, it is impossible to visualize anyone else in the part.

Yet the spell of the movie lies not in its visible characters but in the unseen Rebecca.

It is a well preserved secret until half-way through the story that this implied paragon of feminine grace was not all her successor, the second Mrs de Winter, and we, the audience, have been led to believe. The revelation that Rebecca was a cold-hearted bitch, betraying her husband, planning to abort the child she is expecting, mocking him with her infidelity, never fails in its shock impact.

Rebecca is an icon of the screen's strong, malevolent, dominating women. Even death can't loosen the power and the thrall in which she holds the men in her life.

46

Joan Crawford worked her fingers to the bone for her vicious daughter (Ann Blyth) in Mildred Pierce (above), an anthem to the screen's self-sacrificing mothers.

2

Mother Love

FROM ANY VIEWPOINT the broad landscape of every movie genre is dominated by only a few peaks: a handful of films which, for reasons of quality or popularity, tower above the rest as classics of their kind.

A list of the top-most women's pictures would have to include four distinctive titles, heights of their range: *Stella Dallas*, *Now, Voyager*, *Mildred Pierce* and *Imitation of Life*. Powerfully dramatic, each of them, in its individuality, yet all growing out of a common theme: the mother-child relationship.

Motherhood, good, bad or indifferent, has triggered more anger, anguish, jealousy, heartache and cascading emotion than any other human condition in women's pictures, with the possible exception of war.

Mothers scrimp, scheme and sacrifice for their children. Mothers eat their young with possessiveness and destructive jealousies. Mothers spoil and indulge and manipulate their offspring to feed their maternal vanities and ambitions.

Fathers don't count. Sure, they are known to hover on the sidelines, wringing their hands and observing the strict women's-picture rule that Mother Knows Best. More often, however, they are dead, divorced or have decamped before, or shortly after, the opening credits have rolled. Widows or abandoned wives make the most heartbreaking mothers.

And are the children grateful? Of course they're not. Many a good story-line would have been ruined if they were.

In *Stella Dallas* (1937) Barbara Stanwyck's mill-girl was the prototype mother-love figure — ambitious, self-sacrificing for her daughter's sake and doomed to suffer silently and sadly for it as long as she lived.

Working-class Stella is determined to advance herself by marrying above her station. She snares the suave Stephen Dallas (John Boles), a manager of the local mill and a man with a mystery background. Some time previously he has walked out on his wealthy family and society sweetheart to make a new life for himself after his father's headline-hitting suicide.

Marriage brings Stella all the fancy clothes, home luxuries and social position she has ever day-dreamed of. But breeding will out. Try as she may, she cannot shed the coarse speech and instincts she has grown up with and, happy as both are with their new-born daughter Laurel, the company she insists on keeping puts a strain on the marriage.

Eventually they separate. Laurel stays with her mother in reduced circumstances, visiting regularly with her father as she grows up lovely and ladylike under Stella's tutelage.

He, meanwhile, has been reunited by chance with his old sweetheart (Barbara O'Neil), now a rich widow, and gradually they fall in love again.

Following Stella's well-meant but embarrassing exhibitions of maternal pride during a stay at a swanky hotel, Laurel is shamed into breaking off a promising liaison with a highly eligible Ivy League youth. Stella overhears a group of youngsters ridiculing her dress style and

manners in one of the film's most touchingly affecting moments — beautifully played by Stanwyck — and faces up to her supreme sacrifice.

Pretending indifference to Laurel, claiming she now wants to lead a life of her own and flaunting her vulgarity, she persuades the girl that she will have a better future with her father and his new wife (who alone knows the truth of Stella's heartbreak decision).

Fade-out on one of the most moist scenes in the annals of tear-jerking. Laurel is marrying her Ivy Leaguer amid the luxury of her new home. Stella has disappeared and can't be invited.

Outside in the rain a drab, beshawled figure watches the ceremony through the windows. As the bridal pair kiss, Stella is moved on by a brusque police officer. Her face, raindrops trickling down her cheeks like tears, is transfigured by sorrowing pride.

Barbara Stanwyck desperately wanted the role. Producer Sam Goldwyn had first offered it to Ruth Chatterton, champion mother-figure of 'thirties movies, who had turned it down as being 'too unpleasant'. Gladys George, a recent Oscar nominee, was then considered.

Miss Stanwyck was to say later: 'Goldwyn had flatly refused to consider me because he told me quite frankly that first, he didn't believe I was capable of doing it; second, he thought I was too young; and third, I hadn't enough experience with children.'

Eventually he agreed to let her test — even though she was already a popular star — and the part was hers.

She proceeded to set about it with all the professional zeal that made her name a byword in the studios throughout her career.

She insisted on being de-glamourized, one of the first big-name actresses to risk subordinating her looks for a meaty role. Her figure was padded, her hair cropped and re-styled to achieve a cheap effect; she even stuffed cotton wool inside her cheeks to heighten the blowsy appearance.

By today's standards these cosmetic treatments may seem mild. They were certainly not allowed to impinge too drastically on her familiar features, but it was a daring transformation for those days.

Ultimately, however, it was her expertly shaded acting that earned her the first of her Academy Award nominations (she was up against Greta Garbo for *Camille* and Janet Gaynor for *A Star is Born* and the Oscar went to Luise Rainer for *The Good Earth*). A nomination also came Anne Shirley's way for Best Supporting Actress as Laurel.

The Stanwyck performance is still a showpiece, cleverly balancing the brassy, less appealing traits of the character against the inescapably touching vulnerability of a generous, if misguided, heart.

The author of the original novel *Stella Dallas* was Olive Higgins Prouty, another of whose

48

Barbara Stanwyck suffered similar anguish, though in the cause of an appreciative daughter (Anne Shirley), as the big-hearted woman who could not rise above her vulgar personality, in Stella Dallas (left).

books would result five years later in one of the all-time favourite women's pictures, *Now, Voyager* (1942).

Here again mother-love — or lack of it — was at the root of the drama. By now, thanks in no small measure to Barbara Stanwyck's lead, Hollywood's leading ladies were more confident about shedding their glamour for a role they could sink their teeth into. Even so, it still came as a shock when Bette Davis made her first entrance as Charlotte Vale.

Frumpy in a shapeless frock, she had her hair scraped back unflatteringly into a bun, her eyebrows thickened and coarsened, she wore heavy, unbecoming glasses and no make-up. It was all the fault of a domineering mother!

An unwanted and unloved child, Charlotte had grown up repressed and neurotic, a bond-servant to her selfish mother (and none came more selfish than the splendid Gladys Cooper).

The basic story is the old one of the ugly duckling. Charlotte is treated by a sympathetic psychiatrist (Claude Rains) who as part of his therapy recommends an ocean cruise.

But first a visit to the couturier and the beauty salon. Charlotte, miraculously transformed into the proverbial swan, has a shipboard romance with an unhappily married charmer (Paul Henreid) and in due course returns home with the self-assurance to stand up to her outraged mother.

An uneasy truce between them is worked out but, dead on cue, the dreadful old woman suffers a heart attack and dies, maliciously gratified, one can't help feeling, that Charlotte will live unhappily ever after with a blameless mother's death on her conscience. The screenwriters deemed otherwise, of course, though, to their credit, they avoided the softest available option of marriage between Davis and Henreid in favour of a kind of half-happiness immortalized in her classic fade-out line: 'Oh, Jerry, don't ask for the moon. We have the stars.'

Now, Voyager is, again, an example of base metal fashioned by high-gloss artistry and commitment into gold coinage. In the light of Charlotte's subsequent romantic angst, the mother-daughter theme is only part of the story. But it's the part that counts: the trigger-point for events.

Parallels with *Stella Dallas* extended beyond theme and origin. As Barbara Stanwyck had campaigned for her role, so Bette Davis had to prove herself worthy of Charlotte Vale. The film was originally intended for Irene Dunne. Such is the complete identification of Bette

Bette Davis, after a lifetime of repression from an unloving mother, blossoms under her first experience of romance, with Paul Henreid in Now, Voyager.

Davis with role and film that it is impossible to imagine how any other actress could have been considered. The Oscar nomination she received for her performance was her fifth in successive years.

Miss Davis did not get to play *Mildred Pierce* (1945). Nor did Miss Stanwyck. Both were in line of succession for the part. Joan Crawford was a mere third choice and, at the time, in a severe career trough. But with it she won the only Oscar of her career and found, by default, the role for which she is best remembered.

Like Stella Dallas, Mildred Pierce is a gutsy lady from the bleaker side of the tracks, who hauls herself up the social and economic ladder. Her motivation is slightly different, though. She self-sacrifices for the sake of what must surely be the most vicious ingrate of a daughter the movies ever gave birth to.

While Mildred works her fingers to the bone making a financial success of the restaurant she has founded on tips amassed during her days as a humble waitress, the daughter is scheming to seduce her second husband, eventually shooting him dead when he repudiates her. In the grand tradition of mother-love nobility, no matter how ill-considered, Mildred tries to shield her worthless little darling by taking the rap.

Ann Blyth played the daughter Veda, a character so conceived as to be almost too bad to be true, with a compelling monstrosity that made the palm itch to strike a blow for parental liberation. When, in one of the movie's most celebrated scenes, Mildred does finally slap her, and hard, the release of collective audience frustration is palpable.

Studied dispassionately, though, the characters in *Mildred Pierce* are tokens; pasteboard on which the players can paint their vivid melodramatic colours.

Would any mother as strong and level-headed as Mildred have allowed her favourite child to grow up so irredeemably snobbish, contemptuous and contemptible? Would a daughter have not a single saving grace in her character? And as for the men in their lives — Bruce Bennett as the weak-willed first husband, Zachary Scott as the wealthy, aristocratic second — would they be quite so lacking in backbone?

The answers on all counts are . . . well, yes. The rules of the women's picture decreed it, if for no more practical reason than that the Star Performance demanded it. Miss Crawford, a potent image still in her Milo Anderson-designed tailored suits and matching mink coat and hat, the symbol of material ambition successfully realized, whatever the motive, was the only Man among them.

She had undoubtedly delivered better performances (in *A Woman's Face*, for instance) and her Oscar was probably an industry's laurel wreath for a long and hard-working career rather than a recognition of the year's best acting. But she deserved it for sheer audacity. *Mildred Pierce* jacked her back up there among the greats. It's the apex of an extraordinary career.

From then on for the next twelve years and fifteen movies Joan Crawford would take Mildred Pierce out of the closet and brush her down, shoulders getting progressively squarer,

MOTHER LOVE

Devoted mother Claudette Colbert
in Imitation of Life (below) and
repudiated mother Lana Turner
(right) in Madame X (1966
version).

personality tougher; the dominant factor before whom men cowered or appeased. The women's-picture audience loved it.

Mildred Pierce launched herself on the road to tycoonery by baking and selling home-made cakes. Bea Pullman, the heroine of *Imitation of Life* (1934), got herself started on a similar trail by retailing flapjacks to a secret recipe of her black maid, Aunt Delilah.

Compared with *Mildred Pierce*, *Imitation of Life* has jam on it: a twin-carburettor mother-daughter conflict.

Bea is a gritty widow (aren't they always?) with a daughter; Aunt Delilah, too, is husband-less, with a same-age little girl. And it is the latter little moppet who triggers trouble.

She grows up realizing she can 'pass for white' and, not unreasonably considering the racial hassle she gets from her schoolmates, resolves to do just that by running away from home, getting into low company, rejecting her saintly mother and scorning the poor woman's shame in a daughter who won't face up to the realities of her identity.

Bea, meanwhile, has made a success of flap-jacks but a mess of her maternal career. She and her daughter both wind up in love with the same man, just like Mildred Pierce and Veda.

The screenplay sugared the original novel, by the high priestess of tear-jerking literature, Fannie Hurst, filleting out much of the book's social comment and (for its time) daring observation of racialism and concentrating instead on its high-voltage, more bankable emotionalism.

By the time a broken-hearted Aunt Delilah has pined away and the prodigal daughter has slunk, unbidden and unrecognized, into her funeral service, stricken too late with remorse, no eye in the theatre could be guaranteed dry.

Still, in its own right, *Imitation of Life* is a gem of its kind, 'compulsively watchable' according to Pauline Kael, sincerely meant and played with gossamer sensibilities by Claudette Colbert and Louise Beavers.

Miss Beavers was the regulation black maid of a score of movies in the 'thirties and 'forties. Ironically, she had first arrived in Hollywood as the genuine maid of actress Leatrice Joy in the early days of the silents.

MOTHER LOVE

Nearly a quarter of a century later in 1958 producer Ross Hunter chose *Imitation of Life* to launch his glossy cycle of weepie remakes which succeeded in putting the women's picture on a life-support system during the death throes of its mass appeal.

By then times had changed and so had tastes, gastronomic as well as aesthetic. Flapjacks were out. Bea Pullman and Aunt Delilah were names with dated connotations for sophisticated audiences on the brink of the Swinging Sixties.

They were euphoniously transformed into Lora Meredith and the just-plebeian Annie Johnson. Lora was an actress heading for stardom, thereby justifying a wardrobe Bea Pullman could never had afforded out of flapjacks. Annie remained a maid, albeit with an advance in status to housekeeper.

But apart from such cosmetic touches the foolproof old sob-story was largely respected, given a few deft modernizing corrections to its course. Lora was marginally more career-minded that Bea and accordingly more pointedly neglectful of her maternal duties, though not to the extent of forfeiting sympathy. And, if anything, Annie's light-skinned daughter was harsher, more rebel-without-a-cause, 'fifties-style, as played by Susan Kohner.

Lana Turner, adorned by a reported one-million-dollars'-worth of jewellery, emoted as Lora and steered an ailing career back on to the fast track, much as Joan Crawford had done with *Mildred Pierce*. The role opened up a run of successful women's pictures for her and her bank balance soared, thanks to a deal that gave her half the picture's profits.

The public's response to the movie proved there was still a lot of life left in *Imitation of Life*, 'the most shameless tear-jerker in years', according to the *New York Times*. Reviews, as was to be expected, were generally downbeat but the verdict rested finally with audiences. They rallied to it in such numbers that the production hoisted Universal Studios out of the red.

Juanita Moore, who played Annie Johnson (the singer Pearl Bailey had been considered at one time), and Susan Kohner both rated Best Supporting Actress nominations; and the director Douglas Sirk brought down the curtain on his Hollywood career with all the classiness which now, 30 years later, defines his cult image for the opulent, stylish romances he re-fashioned out of old warhorse weepies.

Of these four key mother-love movies, *Now, Voyager* stands apart. The other three, *Stella Dallas*, *Mildred Pierce* and *Imitation of Life*, all subscribe to and obey the principles of the formula: ambitious, determined mothers; spoiled, wilful daughters, destined for alienating conflict; husbands who are either weak-willed or non-existent; no sons.

Tracking the patterns through mother-love movies reveals a strong preference on the part of screen-writers for 'daughter' subjects — until the Second World War raised sons to hero rank and gave mothers a higher motive for sacrifice.

Any parent with first-hand knowledge will agree that girls are less of a problem to bring up than boys. But the movie melodramatist's preoccupation with 'daughter' characters is not difficult to justify. An ageing mother . . . a flowering daughter . . . rivalry, threat, jealousy!

54

For a female audience programmed to identify with what it is seeing, it's a fail-safe fusion of emotive ingredients.

For all the romantic gloss with which they were so artfully trimmed, the four milestones of mother-love movies remained highlighted in memory by their scenes of confrontation between mother and child.

If daughters were generally spoiled, selfish and vixenish, sons tended to be weak, malleable, tormented by filial duty and loyalty; or lost.

One sure way straight to the heart of the women's picture audience was for a son to be torn by circumstances from his mother's arms in infancy and, by even more unlikely circumstances, restored to her, an adult and a stranger, in time for the fade-out.

There is a fifth peak in the maternal range, *Madame X* (1937). Shamelessly contrived as five-star melodrama, it first reduced Edwardian audiences to tears as a Parisian stage hit in 1909. Hollywood was neither slow nor neglectful in cashing in on its universal popularity.

The first screen version came in 1915 and for the next 50 years, through silent and talkie eras, it was reconstituted four more times. Two of the great mother-stars of women's pictures essayed the role: Pauline Frederick in 1920 and Ruth Chatterton in 1929.

But it was the 1937 version which has remained the definitive edition. Its star was Gladys George, a greatly undervalued actress and now virtually forgotten. That same year she had been under consideration for *Stella Dallas* after Ruth Chatterton turned it down.

No woman has ever suffered more than this unfortunate. As a young, neglected wife, unwelcome in her husband's high-tone family, she embarks on a clandestine romance which is shattered when her lover is accidentally killed on one of their dates.

Repudiated by the family, she flees to Europe rather than bring disgrace on her husband and young son. Over the years she sinks ever deeper into a life of degradation, a succession of sleazy men parading through her boudoir, until one of them involves her in a blackmail scheme. She shoots him when she realizes the intended victim is her long-time-unseen husband.

On trial for murder, her defence is undertaken by a handsome young attorney. And — you guessed it — the lawyer is her grown-up son. Unaware of the true identity of the defendant known in court only as Madame X, he feels strangely drawn to her and gives his all to battle for her acquittal.

Even in its original stage form the subject matter had no pretensions to being other than a blatant manipulative exercise in emotionalism. But as such it was very shrewdly assembled and that, no doubt, accounts for the uncritical, uncomplicated response of tear-stained satisfaction it always drew from those it aimed to please.

It never failed. The last (1966) remake, another sumptuous Ross Hunter extravaganza for Lana Turner, in which the creaking mechanisms of the plot were all too embarrassingly shown up as anachronisms, seduced the London *Evening Standard* critic into an uncharacteristic comment: 'We should be grateful that Hollywood still has the face to make an unabashed weepie with the sluices open.'

MOTHER LOVE

Frances Dee (below) and Joel McCrea, married shortly after appearing together in The Silver Cord, have enjoyed one of Hollywood's most enduring partnerships.

It was perhaps poetic justice that this version virtually brought an end to the women's picture as a genre and Ross Hunter's lucrative lease on them bowed out soggily.

The final curtain was not without some fitting finishing touches of poignancy. Hunter had found supporting roles for two old-timers who had been star stalwarts of 'thirties women's pictures.

He persuaded Constance Bennett out of a twelve-year retirement to play a newly-introduced character, the husband's imperious, aristocratic mother; also brought back was the at one time ubiquitous romantic lead Neil Hamilton, though most of his footage ended on the cutting-room floor.

Miss Bennett, having delivered a ravishing performance, died shortly after production was wrapped. Mr Hamilton would make only two more brief screen appearances, although he would live on until 1984.

The mother (or, more accurately, smother) love factor, as applied to sons, has never been more cogently summed up than in one of the early — but still one of the most effective — talkies, *The Silver Cord* (1933). Indeed, this rarely-aired movie opened up a whole can of sociological worms, also raising a discreet banner in support of a wife's right to work (the ghastly matriarch who dominates the drama welcomes her new daughter-in-law with the invitation: 'Now tell me about your job. I don't like to say profession — that has such a sinister sound for a woman').

This is maggot-mother territory; a monster woman who, under a veneer of caring charm,

Oscar with her first talkie, as a carbon-copy Madame X in *The Sin of Madelon Claudet* (1931; UK title *The Lullaby*), with a 24-year-old Robert Young as the unknowing son in his second screen role.

In a not very convincing switch for *The Secret of Madame Blanche* (1933), it was the son who pulled the trigger and the mother, Irene Dunne, who tried selflessly to take the rap. As an extra unlikely twist, neither of them knew of their blood tie.

Inevitably, ace momma Ruth Chatterton had her turn a second and third time around (she had been the 1929 Madame X). In *Sarah and Son* (1930), directed by Hollywood's only woman director at that time, Dorothy Arzner, she played the long-suffering wife of a no-good man who gives their child away and later dies whispering the name of the foster-parents, the only clue she has to the boy's whereabouts. After a spell in Europe becoming an opera singer, she returns home to trace him with the help of Fredric March, who has fallen in love with her. A similar situation arises in *Frisco Jenny* (1933), in which she is required to hand over her little boy to foster-parents only to find herself, years later, in the dock facing a prosecutor with an uncanny family resemblance. No second guesses as to who! All this and the San Francisco earthquake too.

'To lose one parent, Mr Worthing, may be regarded as a misfortune; to lose both looks like carelessness,' observed Lady Bracknell, who doubtless would have been further bemused by the frequency with which mothers and children misplaced themselves in the movies.

slyly and skilfully burrows under the foundations of her sons' relationships with other women, in one case a wife, in the other a fiancée; a bravura performance by the marvellous Laura Hope Crews (ever to be remembered as Aunt Pittypat in *Gone with the Wind*).

The men, played by Joel McCrea and Eric Linden, are throughout secondary and subordinate to the mother's will, almost cringing in mortification whenever she reminds them of all she has sacrificed for her 'boys' . . . 'and this is how I am rewarded!'

Frances Dee as the fiancée driven to attempt suicide has one telling line which perfectly sums up the entire mother-love syndrome: 'What I say about children is this: have 'em, love 'em, then leave 'em be.'

In the 'thirties, the *Madame X* brand left its mark on a variety of lookalikes. Helen Hayes, First Lady of the American theatre, won an

Irene Dunne (right) played a mother who sought to take the blame for her son's crime in The Secret of Madame Blanche.

Ruth Chatterton, prosecuted by her long-lost lawyer son Donald Cook in Frisco Jenny *(below), and (opposite) falling in love with the lawyer she hires to win back another long-lost child, Fredric March, in* Sarah and Son.

Apart from the Mesdames X, a scheming Loretta Young, having seduced millionaire Cary Grant, was obliged to surrender their love-child to him in *Born to be Bad* (1934) while Ann Harding suffered long on the same tear-stained treadmill in *Gallant Lady* (1934).

This and its remake four years later *Always Goodbye* (1938), with Barbara Stanwyck taking over, involved an unwed mother forced to give her baby for adoption but living in anguished hope of reclaiming the child when the adoptive mother dies prematurely.

Even the glacial Merle Oberon allowed herself to be meltingly maternal in *This Love of Ours* (1945), from a play by Pirandello.

An ex-Parisian showgirl, married to a young going-places doctor (Charles Korvin) at the turn of the century, loses both him and their infant daughter when he erroneously suspects her of adultery. Father and daughter head off for Chicago where ten years later a chance meeting reunites husband and wife. Their reconciliation is complicated — needlessly so — by the problem of making this 'newcomer' wife acceptable to the teenage girl who believes her mother to be dead and has sentimentalized her memory with a shrine in the garden.

The agonizing that follows was, in the view of the *New York Times*, 'about as captivating as a funeral dirge'.

Filming was by all accounts pretty funereal, too. Oberon and Korvin loathed each other. He is quoted in the biography of her by Charles Higham and Roy Moseley:

She was absolutely impossible to work with. She was only interested in her make-up, hair, costumes; she was so overdressed, with elaborate hats, that it was horrible trying to make love to her in a scene . . . She hated the young girl who played her daughter in the picture. She had scenes cut involving the girl because she didn't want to be seen with her as a woman in her thirties.

It says something for Oberon, working in such fraught conditions, that her finished performance was called 'exquisite', even if the film wasn't, by the *New York Times*.

The same story, notwithstanding, was given another whirl during the 1950s gust of second wind (or last gasp) for the women's picture as *Never Say Goodbye* (1956).

Rock Hudson, by now elevated to romantic lead status following his overnight succcess in *Magnificent Obsession*, was more or less required to repeat his character in that movie as the doctor. The beautiful German actress Cornell Borchers played the wife.

New agonies were piled on the old. This time they had met, married and parted for the plot's standard reasons in post-Second World War Vienna. An early attempt at reconciliation had been thwarted by the wife being stranded in the Russian Zone and imprisoned.

The story then gets back on its original tracks for Chicago, where the fortuitous reunion takes place (astounded recognition across a crowded street). Borchers rushes headlong into the traffic and gets knocked down. Her husband performs the necessary operation and saves her

MOTHER LOVE

life. Thus *Never Say Goodbye* received a skin-graft from *Magnificent Obsession*! Only then do the traumas of reuniting mother and daughter commence in earnest.

This was Cornell Borchers' first movie in Hollywood, but a star careeer of which much was expected with the film's release never materialized. After two more, she returned to Germany, where her intelligence as an actress was more highly appreciated.

So back to displaced sons and *To Each His Own* (1946), which is typical of the superior, well-crafted Hollywood product, popular with its audiences yet critically undervalued because of its 'weepie' provenance.

Nevertheless it earned Olivia de Havilland the first of her two Academy Awards and another for Charles Brackett's stylish, all-stops-out screenplay. On the debit side, in terms of deserving to be taken seriously, it also offered a theme song which became a gigantic hit. Nothing in those days could be more calculated to debase and vulgarize a seriously intended picture.

Told mainly in flashback, it presents a middle-aged Miss de Havilland as an air-raid warden in London during the Blitz recalling a youthful love affair in the previous war.

The man had been killed in action and she gives birth to an illegitimate son whom she allows to be adopted. Inevitably, the boy, now a war-hero duplicate of his father, re-enters her lonely life not realizing who she is until the fade-out.

John Lund ambidextrously played both father and son, thereby repeating a trick patented years earlier by Ruth Chatterton when

'Impossible' Merle Oberon was jealous of her screen daughter in This Love of Ours.

she had doubled as mother and daughter in *The Right to Live*.

One bizarre footnote to this production, revealed by Charles Higham in his biography *Olivia and Joan*, is that de Havilland's ageing make-up was modelled on a magazine picture-spread of Sir Winston Churchill at different stages of his life!

If a general rule can be drawn to apply to mother-love subjects, it seems to be that sons and daughters are equal causes of anguish and heartbreak but with a clearly defined difference. Sons are unwitting instruments of motherly troubles; daughters, by their very nature and feminine challenge, incite it deliberately.

In the thrice-filmed *So Big* (1932), most durable of all mother-son plots, the word recurringly used to describe the effect on the selfless, hard-working widow-heroine of her beloved son's failure to live up to expectations is 'disappointment'. There's nothing stronger than that!

It is not that he's bad or unappreciative, just unmotivated. She dreams of his becoming an architect; he opts for a less prestigious job as a salesman and also for the blandishments of a married woman.

Mother, in her disappointment, diverts her idealism to a friend's son who has become a famous sculptor and who tells her (rather unctuously) that her noble ideals have been his inspiration. This, presumably, is the answer to a mother's prayer, at least in the Hollywood form of worship.

Finally, the real son takes up (more by good luck than good judgement, one feels) with a

Good Woman who sympathizes with his mother's principles and gives her reason to believe the girl may succeed where she herself has failed in making a man of him.

Barbara Stanwyck's performance, in the nature of a dry run for *Stella Dallas* five years later, was deemed by the *New York World-Telegram* at the time to establish her 'as a brilliant emotional actress'. An *ingénue* Bette Davis played the redeeming girlfriend and George Brent made the first impact of his Hollywood career as the young sculptor — the first of many screen partnerships Davis and Brent would enjoy.

The popular Edna Ferber novel, first filmed in 1925 with Colleen Moore, was accorded four-handkerchief treatment again in 1953, launching Jane Wyman, in a highly regarded performance, on her cycle of lush tear-jerkers which would briefly bring a late re-flowering of the women's picture.

Ross Hunter, the power behind it, introduced one quirky new dimension to the old formula. He delighted in piling on the agony for his mother characters by using entire broods of children to promote domestic disharmony.

Reversing the usual trend, it was the mother who was 'lost', or long gone missing, in *All I Desire* (1953).

Barbara Stanwyck has walked out on her decent but stodgy schoolmaster husband and their children ten years earlier (the period is the early 1900s) to fulfil her ambition to become a great actress before time runs out on her.

While working tenth-rate vaudeville halls, too proud to admit failure and crawl back home, she gets a letter from her younger daughter who, believing mother to be a star, is determined to follow in her footsteps. The girl is to perform in a school production and begs her to come back just this once to see her act.

Miss Stanwyck, proud and unrepentant, duly turns up to the consternation of a hostile elder daughter, husband's current girlfriend (who is banking on marriage) and sundry small-town scandalmongers.

Being Stanwyck, she admits forthrightly to the errors of her previous ways and busies herself restoring the disoriented family to an even keel. This process happens to necessitate

accidentally shooting the local Lothario, whose attentions had been a factor in her decison to run away in the first place.

Her major battle, though, is with the disapproving elder child whose respect she must win back.

Miss Stanwyck was again the cause of family strife in *There's Always Tomorrow* (1956), a mild remake of an already mild 1933 original. She plays an old flame who by chance comes back into Fred MacMurray's life and is gently persuaded to get lost again by his busybody kids, thus sparing their mother Joan Bennett from ever knowing how treacherously Dad has been rocking the domestic boat.

These two movies, entertaining enough in their modest ways, marked the low point of Barbara Stanwyck's movie career. Soon she would turn to television and make a name for herself all over again with the long-running western series *The Big Valley*.

Easily the most obnoxious brood of children Ross Hunter ever assembled were Jane Wyman's in *All That Heaven Allows* (1956). One of the earliest movies bold enough to depict a genuine love-match, as distinct from a sex-game, between a middle-aged woman and a considerably younger man, it was a popular success.

Widowed Miss Wyman falls for the strapping young guy who drops by occasionally to tidy her garden — thereby gratifying a worldwide female wish-fulfilment since he took the form of Rock Hudson.

The beautiful German actress Cornell Borchers.

*After a series of minor comedy
roles Jane Wyman became the
cinema's top tear-jerker in films
such as* All That Heaven Allows.

Her life is made a misery when she takes up with confirmed womanizer George Brent too soon after mourning her husband's death and her hithero unsullied reputation is shredded by a braying pack of socialite acquaintances led by her own mother. Critics, as might be expected, loathed it but they didn't deter Stanwyck fans, who flocked to it.

It is one of life's tragic ironies that Barbara Stanwyck, so motherly in her fictional roles, was fated to be unsuccessful in her real-life one. She never had children of her own but adopted a son, Dion, during her first marriage, to Broadway star Frank Fay, in the early 1930s. The relationship between them seems always to have been a difficult one and for more than 30 years now they have never communicated.

She was one of the few glamour stars unafraid to be cast in mother roles. Many fought shy of them on grounds of 'image'.

Bette Davis gave birth to a baby in *Of Human Bondage* (1934) and had a son in *That Certain Woman* (1937). But following a miscarriage in *The Sisters* (1938), brought on by the San Francisco earthquake, which has a lot to answer for, she opted for surrogate motherhood during the glory days of her reign in women's pictures.

In *The Old Maid* (1939), perhaps the most poignant of them, her illegitimate daughter is adopted by her cousin, Miriam Hopkins. The child grows up calling Miss Hopkins 'Mother' and the old maid Miss Davis 'Aunt'.

It's hardly to be wondered the girl has identity problems, since all three of them end up living under the same roof with 'Aunt', reasonably enough, instinctively trying to impose a

Not that this counted with her teenaged offspring. Selfish and snobbish, they try to wreck the romance as much for reasons of social status as of unbecoming age difference. The situation gave rise to at least one fondly remembered scene when Miss Wyman finally rounds on her children and tells them exactly what she — and the rest of us — thinks of them.

In view of her track record it seems only fair that the indomitable Barbara Stanwyck should take the credit for achieving the decathlon of mother-love clichés.

In *My Reputation* (1946), which she is on record as citing one of her favourite movies, she played a composite of widow, mother (of two small sons) and daughter (of a domineering mother).

proper parental discipline on her and being rewarded only with resentment and hatred. Never did Miss Davis suffer more nobly or conceal her secret heartache more affectingly.

In *All This and Heaven Too* (1940) she was the much-loved governess to the children of the Duc de Pralin (Charles Boyer) and his cold-hearted duchess. Parisian high society is deliciously scandalized when the duchess dies in mysterious circumstances and the duke and governess, suspected of a backstairs love affair, are both accused of murder.

Miss Davis herself thinks up *The Great Lie* (1941) to mislead her one true love, George Brent, into not suspecting that the son she has adopted is in fact his child by the ambition-ridden concert pianist (Mary Astor) for whom he originally jilted Davis, and whose all-consuming career will be hindered by the demands of motherhood.

Even in *Now, Voyager* Davis contrives to turn her own repressed daughterhood to caring advantage, by appointing herself as substitute mother to the troubled child of the man she loves.

When after many years she again permitted herself to have a child of her own in *Mr Skeffington* (1944), she repudiated her until she was ageing and the girl grown up.

'I know you had a difficult choice to make,' vain Fanny Skeffington is told by her daughter. 'You couldn't be both a beauty and a mother.'

Davis 'mothered' a brilliant but uneducated Welsh miner as the schoolma'am in *The Corn is Green* (1945) and, widowed and childless, 'adopted' the entire juvenile population of her

Claude Rains, fated to be typecast as the older, unloved husband, was never more shabbily treated than by Bette Davis in Mr Skeffington *(above). Vanity even prompted her to disavow her daughter, Marjorie Riordan (below).*

community as the idealistic librarian in *Storm Centre* (1956).

Furnished by the scriptwriters with a family of daughters in *Payment on Demand* (1951), the anatomy of a divorce, she impishly slipped her own child Barbara Merrill into the cast to portray one of them.

With so many parallels and points of reference between the careers of Bette Davis and Joan Crawford, it could be providential that as real-life mothers they should both be savaged in print by their daughters.

Little Barbara Merrill, so cuddlesome in *Payment on Demand*, grew up to be Barbara Hyman, author of the 1985 book *My Mother's Keeper*, a distressful 'portrait' of Bette Davis in the same mould as Christina Crawford's hatchet-job on her mother in *Mommie Dearest*.

Joan Crawford had only been a screen mother once, in *Susan and God* (1940), before she accepted — not without misgivings — her Oscar-winning Mildred Pierce role as the mother of a grown-up daughter.

Crawford's monster-mother was enshrined on film by Faye Dunaway in *Mommie Dearest* (1981). The Davis martyrdom will no doubt follow in due course.

Not, at first sight, the most motherly of women, Marlene Dietrich nevertheless had no inhibitions about taking on a maternal role (nor, come to that, later being dubbed 'the world's most glamorous grandmother'). Soon after her arrival in Hollywood she suffered the obligatory agonies and degradations in the cause of bringing up her son decently in *Blonde Venus* (1932).

The child actor in this case was 7-year-old Dickie Moore, one of the most in demand during the 'thirties, whose screen mothers also included Barbara Stanwyck and Ann Harding. A decade later he would achieve movie immortality of sorts by giving Shirley Temple her first screen kiss in *Miss Annie Rooney*.

Lana Turner, the perennial Sweater Girl, admits to taking a metaphorical deep breath before accepting a mother role — her first — in *Peyton Place* (1957). This steamy but stylish chronicle of love tangles in a small New England town required her to have an illegitimate teenage daughter.

'To play the mother of an 18-year-old girl was a radical departure for me,' she wrote in her autobiography, 'but the script was too tempting to turn down.'

In the event the risk was more than justified. Her performance merited an Oscar nomination, just as taking the plunge into motherhood had done for Joan Crawford in *Mildred Pierce*.

But Turner's moment of glory was to be sensationally overshadowed by a real-life mother-daughter melodrama of her own.

Her 14-year-old daughter Cheryl accompanied her to the Academy Award ceremony on 26 March 1958. Ten days later on 5 April Cheryl plunged a kitchen knife into the stomach of her mother's gangster lover Johnny Stompanato after hearing him threaten to 'cut up' the star. The killing made headlines around the world for weeks.

Hollywood would hardly have dared invent such a scenario but it had no scruples about battening on to Harold Robbins's *roman-à-clef* which, despite the author's disavowals, bore a marked resemblance to the case.

In *Where Love Has Gone* (1964) Susan Hayward portrayed a sculptress whose lover is stabbed to death by her disturbed 15-year-old daughter. The character of Hayward's mother in the story was played by Bette Davis, who in real life was a mere ten years older.

MOTHER LOVE

Lana Turner and her daughter Cheryl Crane
attended the Academy Awards (opposite) in 1958
when Lana was nominated for playing her first
mother role in Peyton Place with Diana Varsi (left).
Ten days after the Awards Cheryl stabbed her
mother's lover to death, a news sensation which
inspired Where Love Has Gone with Susan Hayward
(below).

HEDY LAMARR

MOTHER LOVE

'The world's most beautiful woman', Hedy Lamarr, effectively ended her career by playing the mother of a grown-up daughter. The Female Animal, in which her co-star was George Nader, was the last movie she ever made.

There is a macabre reminder of that traumatic episode for Lana Turner if ever she chances to see *Peyton Place* on television. The jewellery she wore in it was her own — the gift of Johnny Stompanato.

It probably required even more courage than Turner's for another screen goddess to own to a grown-up daughter that same year. Hedy Lamarr was, after all, generally acknowledged to be the Most Beautiful Woman in Movies (some claimed in the world).

The film was *The Female Animal* (1957). It was fairly dire but its consequences for its three leading players proved even worse.

Lamarr was cast as a glamorous film star on the wane who is saved from a serious accident on set by the quick thinking of a handsome young extra (George Nader). She falls in love with him and gives him a job as caretaker at her beach house in order to keep him handy.

Picking up a young woman one night, he takes her back to the house, not knowing she is the star's daughter. In this role MGM's popular singing star Jane Powell made an undistinguished dramatic début. She was 28 at the time, sixteen years Lamarr's junior.

Competition between mother and daughter for the man (ironic in the light of subsequent revelations about George Nader) is complicated by a third female party, another film star, taking an interest in him.

The Female Animal was the last film Hedy Lamarr and Jane Powell were ever to make and was to be Nader's Hollywood swansong.

He was homosexual. Universal, which had him on contract, was paranoid about a threatened newspaper exposé of the off-screen activities of its top male star Rock Hudson. They struck a deal with the paper to sacrifice Nader for a scandal-sheet spread in return for hushing up the Hudson story, and Nader was self-exiled to low-grade European films which ultimately brought him some consolation as a minor screen idol in West Germany.

Legend has it that Norma Shearer turned down the role of *Mrs Miniver*, a movie that would have given her declining career a spectacular boost, because she was apprehensive about playing the mother of three children, one a grown-up son.

The part went to Greer Garson, confirming her accession to Miss Shearer's title as 'gracious first lady of the screen' and culminating in probably the most bizarre spin-off of movie motherhood. Soon after production was completed Miss Garson married her screen 'son' Richard Ney, who at 25 was ten years her junior. They were divorced four years later.

Foot-of-the-stairs note: the most appalling mother-who-never-was must surely have been Gene Tierney in *Leave Her to Heaven*.

Pathologically jealous of anyone who comes between her and her husband, she kills her unborn child by deliberately falling downstairs rather than risk the prospect of its distracting his love from her.

3

The Other Woman

IN *NOW, VOYAGER* the recently liberated Charlotte Vale withholds her true identity at first from the married man who is to become her great love, so he gives her the nickname Camille. When they are apart subsequently he regularly sends her camellias, which she wears as a corsage, mystifying friends and relations with their significance.

Discreetly and proudly, she is telling the world and reminding herself that she wears the badge of the mistress: the true love of a man who belongs to someone else.

Alexandre Dumas Fils created the symbol of the camellia to represent illicit sexual love. In *The Lady of the Camellias* he raised the mistress to a status of romantic lyricism and near-respectability.

It was somehow very right and, yes, proper that the goddess of cinema Greta Garbo should play the title role in *Camille*, the definitive mistress movie.

Camille, by the very nature of her calling, cannot be beyond reproach. But in the light of her obvious integrity and self-sacrificing nobility, who will dare cast the first stone?

The memorable movie mistresses have all had this quality, this shadow of tragedy, in common. It is, after all, dramatically foolproof, exploiting the old governing rule of audience identification.

No woman with a man of her own welcomes or condones a mistress; a rival. But her heart will go out to the 'other woman' whose sincerity, honesty and patient fortitude console a man stuck with an unloving, unloved wife. She, too,

would be that sort of mistress in the same circumstances.

Camille's Armand was not, in fact, already married; the challenge she represented as a 'kept woman' was to the social standing of his family and, specifically, to that of his soon-to-be-wed sister.

But, then, none of the great mistress characters of the movies has been an out-and-out husband-stealer. That would never do!

On the contrary they are invariably innocents, victims of overpowering emotion, caught up in a destiny not of their own making but, once snared, committed to easing the pain of their man's unhappiness or frustration. Each is a mistress *de facto* . . . but not mistress of her own fate.

Hackneyed as its story is through repetition in virtually every medium from opera to parody, *Camille* transcends the standard expectations of a woman's picture by virtue of Garbo's luminous performance.

In Gavin Lambert's book *On Cukor* the film's director George Cukor recalled:

> I'd seen the play and I felt it would be a perfect meeting of the actress and the role. Certain people are born to play certain parts.

How right he was. *Camille*, half a century later, remains Garbo's best-remembered role, character and film. She drenched all three with the unique essence of her aura.

As production was in preparation MGM anticipated possible trouble with the Hays Office, guardians of filmgoers' morals in those days.

Greta Garbo and Robert Taylor in
Camille *(opposite).*

71

THE OTHER WOMAN

This was, after all, a story that celebrated a woman of dubious morals and more or less sanctified her.

Probably no mistress but Garbo was capable of conveying, without needing to enact, the banked fires of sensuality which the role required but which would have given the censors cause to intervene. As Cukor described her, 'She could let [the audience] know she was thinking things, and thinking them uncensored.'

For Pauline Kael 'Garbo's artistry triumphs and the tear-jerker *Camille* is transformed into the "classic" the studio claimed it to be'. And she adds: 'No movie has ever presented a more romantic view of a courtesan.'

Camille stands in a class of its own, a cinema legend. Whenever it is revived for a Garbo season it is the title that still draws the biggest crowds.

No producer dared remake it — the comparison was doomed to be odious — until a television company took the risk in 1985. Nor have there been the straight cribs from its theme as so many successful originals have tended to spawn a clutch of lookalikes.

Curiously, though, Garbo himself did not come entirely fresh to the part. Two of her early talkies can be seen in hindsight to have been in the nature of trial runs for it.

In *Romance* (1930), her second talkie, she played a prima donna with whom a young priest falls in love. She deserts her wealthy protector for him but the priest, jealously misinterpreting a meeting she has with her former lover in which she has refused to return to him,

denounces her just as the equally misunderstanding Armand humiliates Camille for similar reasons. When the priest begs her to spend one last night with him before they part, she implores him not to treat her in the way men before him always had.

Years later (the story is told in flashback), the priest, now a bishop, learns of her death while he is telling his grandson the story in an attempt to dissuade the young man from marrying an actress. One critic of Garbo wrote:

> Her performance is a thing of pure beauty, an inspiring blend of intellect and emotion, a tender, poignant, poetic portrait of a woman who thrusts love from her because she considers herself unworthy of the man who offers it.

Camille exactly!

Garbo's next movie, *Inspiration* (1931), was even nearer the mark with its tale of an artist's model ardently wooed by a young man of superior class (Robert Montgomery) who is unaware of her previous lovers. He deserts her but, like Armand, returns to find one of her ex-lovers has taken up with her again.

When he vows to give up his promising career in the diplomatic service for her she waits until he is asleep then walks out of his life rather than ruin it.

'*Camille* without the cough' was how the *New York Times* summed it up.

Two years after Camille the theme surfaced, somewhat timidly, in *The Shopworn Angel* (1938), though it owed less to Dumas and *The Lady of the Camellias* than to a successful 1929 vehicle for Gary Cooper and Nancy Carroll (technically a silent, both stars were heard to speak for the first time in its final scene).

Now James Stewart and Margaret Sullavan (inheriting a role intended for Joan Crawford) played the simple First World War soldier and tarnished actress whose romance picked a bitter-sweet path through the minefield of her wealthy former lovers.

The piquant Miss Sullavan had, at this time, recently become a favourite women's-picture symbol of self-sacrifice. Her finest heartbreak hour was to come three years later in *Back Street* (1941).

What *Madame X* was to mother-love, *Back Street* was to mistress movies — a minor cottage industry. The best-selling novel by *Imitation of Life* author Fannie Hurst had been published in 1931 and promptly bought for the screen. Here was gritty/romantic twentieth-century emotionalism descended from *The Lady of the Camellias* but far removed from her poetic lyricism.

It is the story of Ray Schmidt, a generous-hearted girl from the poor German quarter of Cincinatti, unwanted by her parents, allowed to run wild and consequently no better than she should be, until she meets the wealthy banker Walter Saxel.

Their love is life-long but with one intractable complication. He is married and ever shall be. He can't, won't or daren't get a divorce for fear of compromising his professional and social standing.

This is not a character weakness so much as a literary slyness in the original writing. Fannie Hurst was shrewd enough to know that the female psyche would accept, even forgive, any number of disagreeable faults in a man so long as he was basically kindly and loyal to the woman he truly loves. And that, if no other finer quality, can certainly be attributed to Walter Saxel. No matter what vicissitudes beset and separate them, he always returns to his mistress.

She, meanwhile, with his financial backing, has carved out a successful one-woman business of her own and settled for living out her days in the 'back streets' of his life and love, the kept woman who is content to pick up such crumbs as her man allows to fall from the respectable table of his life-style.

The first film version of 1932, a year after the book's publication, proved to be that rare case of an undistinguished though immensely popular original destined to be outclassed by a remake, the 1941 Margaret Sullavan version. Irene Dunne was a sensitive Ray to the Walter of John Boles, a handsome but wooden matinée idol who enjoyed a durable popularity through the 'thirties specializing in this type of role.

Even so he deserved pity. Walter Saxel is one of the most thankless characters ever allocated to a romantic male lead. Weak, selfish, indecisive, he has few redeeming features except a willingness to part with money sufficient to keep his mistress in a modestly comfortable style. Yet the actor playing him is expected to divine some sympathetic traits if he is to win and hold credibility with a women's audience.

Not that John Boles need have felt too aggrieved by the unsympathetic nature of the

THE OTHER WOMAN

The longest-suffering 'other woman' was the heroine of Back Street. *Three versions spanned three decades, furnishing fail-safe weepie roles for Margaret Sullavan (right) in 1932 and Irene Dunne, with John Boles, in 1941 (opposite).*

role. It enabled him to build his mini-career playing carbon-copy types in subsequent variations on the *Back Street* theme.

The success of the 1941 remake was, however, quite another story.

Even the critics approved this time, albeit tempering praise with the obligatory brush-off for its 'women's picture' pedigree.

The movie was half-way to a hit, sight unseen, by casting Charles Boyer as Walter. Mr Boyer started with the advantage over John Boles of being a fine actor. Moreover he had the refinement at his fingertips for tipping the audience's sympathy towards the more romantic qualities in a character whatever else it left to be desired. With Boyer, these qualities were, in any case, all his women fans wanted to desire, lulled as they were by the subtle Gallic devices of his voice, eyes and accent.

Miss Sullavan's personality, too, was the perfect complement for him; a winning mix of spontaneity and sincerity layered with a sense of good humour.

This, then, was teaming which produced the required chemistry at just the right strength and lifted their *Back Street* clear of sentimentality while preserving its sentiments.

John Boles, meanwhile, had gone wandering about side alleys leading off Back Street. Within months, cresting the wave of the film's success two years earlier, he had permutated its theme twice over. The sources for both these movies were novels by esteemed writers who were doubtless a trifle nonplussed to find how their books had been studio-processed and repackaged into facsimiles of *Back Street*.

The Life of Vergie Winters (1934), based on a Louis Bromfield novel, enrolled the saintly Ann Harding to bide tenderly for 20 years, sacrificing all other chances of happiness for a wealthy Mr Boles who could not extricate himself from a vindictive wife. The screws were, if anything, turned even more tightly on her than on Ray Schmidt; she relinquishes their daughter rather than expose her to the unrelenting campaign of vilification good society used to heap on the heads of kept women in those days.

John Boles and Irene Dunne were reunited for *The Age of Innocence* (1934) but their

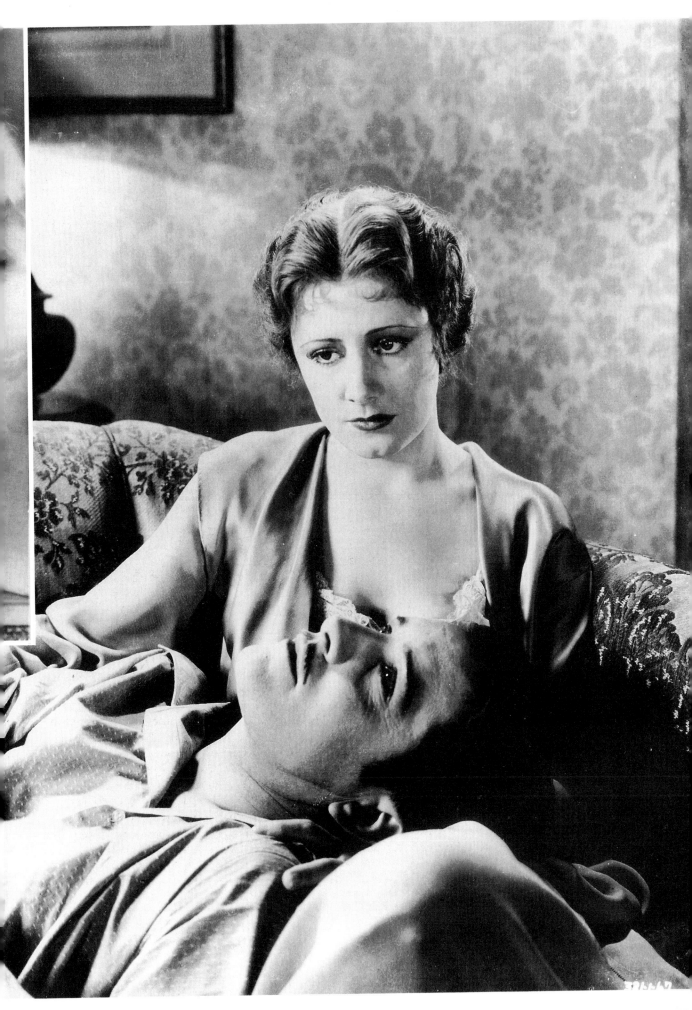

THE OTHER WOMAN

A rare detour out of screwball comedy cast Carole Lombard (right) as a troubled mistress in In Name Only.

A stylish Susan Hayward took Back Street *up-market for its glossy third reincarnation (opposite).*

partnership failed to rekindle the sparks of their *Back Street* success. Edith Wharton's novel, published in 1920 and acknowledged now (but not then) as a minor classic, was concerned in the broad sense with Victorian values and the hypocrisies stemming from them of Old New York society.

Little of her acute sociological observation made the transition from page to film. Instead the screenplay concentrated on the plot mechanics of a doomed love-affair between the stars: she a woman of distinction in the process of divorce and thereby courting social banishment; he, eternally obsessed with her, marrying another but constantly returning for ever more emotional punishment. She it is, of course, who makes the ultimate grand gesture of sacrifice by sending him back finally to his wife.

The mantle of these careworn, not to say by now shopworn, emotions was inherited by an unlikely pair, Carole Lombard and Cary Grant, in *In Name Only* (1939).

Both stars were already established as beacons of light/screwball comedy, so their fans must have been slightly disconcerted by this oddball casting in a highly charged emotional drama.

Despondency abounded. So, come to that, did coincidence. Miss Lombard played a sad-eyed but spunky young widow who rents a summer cottage in Connecticut and keeps crossing paths with Mr Grant, the local landed gentleman who is her landlord. Gently they fall in love.

Inevitably, she also crosses paths with his wife, chancing to be on hand when the lady,

identity blissfully unsuspected, is involved in a car crash outside the cottage.

No fool, this wife, but Kay Francis in one of her icy, ungiving and unforgiving moods. Realizing what is going on behind her back, she blocks her husband's request for a divorce by threatening to sue his new mistress for alienation of affections.

Miss Lombard resigns herself to the pre-ordained life in a back street of love, but pneumonia comes to the rescue. Mr Grant catches it while wandering the icy streets after a monumental showdown with Miss Francis. As the two women converge on his hospital sickbed, almost but not quite a deathbed, the one's caring devotion and the other's vicious

selfishness are displayed in their true colours. True love triumphs.

The light touch at which all three stars were so skilled was their, and the film's, salvation. There is a considered realism in their playing of characters written with an unsubtle hand. The movie, handsomely directed and photographed, scored heavily as a result — 'a classy, not a first-class picture', according to Graham Greene's review.

After *In Name Only* the *Back Street* industry reverted to the prototype. No more replicas, but the 1941 remake and then again a re-remake in 1961.

Ross Hunter dusted off the old warhorse this time, buffing it up into a glossy, wholly artifi-

cial but still fail-safe popular version with Susan Hayward and John Gavin. This was a cosmetic treatment, absolutely typical of its exploitive period. Ray Schmidt was now trendily re-named Rae Smith and transformed into a jet-setting high-achieving fashion designer. Walter Saxel became the more dashing Paul Saxon and traded the old stuffy banker image for that of heir to a department-store fortune. It was hard to conceive of the short-fused, independent-minded Susan Hayward sitting out her days compliantly while a featureless John Gavin vacillated over divorce. The film was entertaining enough — and a box-office hit — on its own terms but they were no longer those of the original *Back Street*.

One other movie carried strong resonances of the theme but strictly on its own terms. *Carrie* (1952) was based on *Sister Carrie*, the first novel, published in 1900, of Theodore Dreiser, a giant of American literature.

Its story reverses the *Back Street* process. It is the wealthy lover, not his kept woman, who suffers in hopeless patience and self-sacrifice.

The film is distinguished by having Laurence Olivier in a role he surprised friends and admirers by accepting at that high point of his career. He made no bones about his motives for doing so. The money was needed and production coincided with that of *A Streetcar Named Desire*, thus enabling him and his wife Vivien Leigh to be working in Hollywood at the same time.

The title role went to Jennifer Jones.

Carrie was a commercial flop; a movie which then and since has been overlooked and underrated. Slow and slightly ponderous, it was directed by William Wyler in his characteristically ornate, conscientious style and proved to be a fairly scrupulous adaptation of the novel.

But its all-the-way-downbeat story with a disposition of unrelieved tragedy didn't appeal.

Carrie is a country girl, honest and hardworking, trying to make her own way in Chicago, who is taken up by the urbane, well-heeled restaurant manager Hurstwood.

When the secret of his kept woman is exposed, his world crashes round his ears. He loses his job and his shrewish wife (a splendid study in venom by Miriam Hopkins) refuses him a divorce.

Setting up home together, the lovers slide into hard times and deepening despair. Hurstwood's sense of failure moves him to break with Carrie so that she can fulfil her dreams unencumbered by him. She keeps searching for him in vain while developing a stage career; he meanwhile has plumbed the depths of degradation.

One night at the stage door she notices a tramp-like figure watching her from the shadows. It is Hurstwood, wracked with illness — a broken man. Still loving him, she takes him to her dressing-room, joyfully assuring him she is now in a position to care for him. But knowing this to be another of her dreams, he quietly slips out of her life for good while she is absent from the room.

Few films have ended more poignantly and, indeed, William Wyler consistently drew out

Laurence Olivier gave one of his most sensitive screen performances as the businessman ruined by his illicit passion for Jennifer Jones in Carrie (opposite).

the qualities of the book and of the players: Jennifer Jones movingly sensitive to the delicacies of her character, Olivier admirably restrained in perhaps the least showy of his leading screen roles. *Carrie* is an unacknowledged model of the quality emotion picture.

If historians of the future look to the movies as barometers of socio-moral codes and trends they could be forgiven for jumping to a conclusion that the world and his wife in the 1930s were unmitigated adulterers.

Film characters of both sexes were habitually careering off the rails and making a deceptively soft landing in the illicit arms of a third party.

None more than Kay Francis. Her stony-hearted wife in *In Name Only* was the last fanfare of a dazzlingly popular career. It was already on the skids at that point and her old friend Carole Lombard, ever the generous one, used her studio clout to secure the role for her.

Kay Francis was one of those comparatively few stars admired equally by men and women fans, much as Marilyn Monroe would be later. Tall, dark and ultra-sophisticated, she was also capable of generating a warmth and wit when required which appealed to men. Women could appreciate those qualities too, with the bonus for them of an independent spirit and, probably the deciding factor in her allure, a faultless instinct for wearing high fashion.

Her dress sense was impeccable. In terms of couture Miss Francis was the quintessential 'thirties fashion-plate.

One of her frequent co-stars, Herbert Marshall, eulogized her thus in a 1933 fan magazine:

She'll spend hours and hours over a fitting for a screen costume. Nothing but the 'absolutely right' will satisfy her. She looks beautiful in anything and knows how to wear her clothes and make them seem part of her. Off the screen she goes in a great deal for tweeds, tailored things, simply but perfectly cut. Her taste in clothes is really exquisite.

There was, however, a small Achilles heel — or near enough to one — in this perfection, as star photographer John Engstead revealed a few years after her death in 1968 at the age of 65:

An unusual, striking beauty, she stood five feet nine inches tall, wore size two shoes and consequently was very unsteady on her feet. Once while filming *Raffles* with Ronald Colman she made an impressive entrance down a marble staircase. When she arrived at the bottom she tripped and fell flat on her face. 'Damned little feet,' she said.

A roll-call of titles is sufficient to place the kind of movie that gave Kay Francis her popularity: *Passion Flower*, *A Notorious Affair*, *The Virtuous Sin*, *Transgression*, *I Loved a Woman*, *Give Me Your Heart*, *Confession*.

She was shrewd in her manipulation of roles, alternating between mistress, usually of a sympathetic stripe, and wronged but still-loving wife. No actress ever hedged her bets more astutely. She even ventured to portray Florence Nightingale in *The White Angel*, acquitting herself creditably if a little self-consciously. And she was expert at comedy.

Her career peaked in 1937 when she was one of Hollywood's highest-paid stars, earning $227,000 a year. Her eclipse came about with the rise at Warner Brothers, her studio, of Bette Davis, who began to corner the role market Miss Francis had dominated.

The Sisters had originally been intended for her — and she begged in vain to play the Empress Carlotta in *Juarez*. Both parts went to Bette Davis. And when, shortly afterwards, she left the studio for good, humiliated and embittered, it was Miss Davis who moved into her star dressing-room.

The final act of her career was not without a certain pathos. In the mid-1940s she tried to rekindle former glories by producing her own starring vehicles. Their titles had a familiar, far-away ring about them: *Divorce*, *Allotment Wives*, *Wife Wanted*. But they were inferior, low-budget afterwords to what had gone before and the public was no longer interested.

Few of her movies are remembered now. None was destined to become a classic. But whether as mistress or wife Kay Francis is inseparable from film styles of the 'thirties, the great age of the women's picture — and the embodiment of their fashion style, avidly studied and copied by women the world over.

She was, however, the victim of changing styles in story values. As the Second World War drew nearer and the world grew increasingly aware that dangerous times lay ahead the taste for inconsequential, all-but-frivolous adultery soured. Serious conditions called for more serious themes.

The first emotional drama to acknowledge,

Kay Francis, often 'the other woman', always glamorous.

however obliquely, the prevailing forces of that war-shadowed period was *We Are Not Alone* (1939).

Paul Muni, in what he was always to refer to as his favourite role, played a gentle, inoffensive doctor in an English cathedral city, married to a shrewish wife (Flora Robson), who falls in love with a much younger refugee from Austria (Jane Bryan). Their tender affair comes under a merciless public spotlight when he is accused of his wife's murder.

Distancing itself from its times, the film — 'of rare tenderness and beauty', according to the *New York Times* — was set on the eve of the previous war. Even so, the presence in it of a heroine bidding for sympathy who was Austrian and a prospective enemy did not find favour with audiences and the film undeservedly failed. Nowadays on its rare screenings its qualities can be better appreciated, particularly the measured, well-judged performances of its stars and the affecting sensitivity of Edmund Goulding's direction.

If, as we have already seen, Bette Davis was adept at mothering without noticeably being a mother, she was equally fastidious in the role of mistress.

It was rare to witness her actually carrying out the duties of one; even in *All This and Heaven Too* her governess's relationship with the Duc is enigmatic and only inferred by the more pruriently suspicious minds in the audience.

But mistress she indisputably was from time to time. The famous opening scene of *The Letter* (1940) shows her pumping bullets into the man who has just advised her he no longer wishes to retain her services as a mistress. Subsequently her latent dedication to those services hangs subtly but unstated like a pall over the drama that follows. The defence that she was protecting her 'honour' as a faithful wife to Herbert Marshall while he was away from home crumbles when the letter of the title is produced, a letter she had written to the man she killed, and unmistakably penned by a mistress.

At the beginning of *Mr Skeffington* the ageing Fanny, setting us up for flashback, descends a staircase to the admiring, nay ogling, attention of a group of old flames. Has she been the kept woman of all or any of them? Two hours later, in the final scene, Fanny chirrups: 'A woman is beautiful only when she is loved', with a wealth of innuendo. But we can only guess what that skittish remark implies.

In *Now, Voyager* she recounts to her psychiatrist the story of 'a friend' — herself, as we well know — who had once found herself stranded throughout the night with a man — the one she loves, as we well know — and allowed her inhibitions to slip. There is no

room for doubt that she is Paul Henreid's mistress through most of the movie. But not once are they so much as glimpsed *in flagrante*.

She had been Claude Rains' mistress when *Deception* (1946) opens but the stress is on the past tense as she re-discovers her old love for Paul Henreid, a cellist just returned from the dead.

Rains, a composer, invites the man who has usurped him, now her husband, to perform the solo part in his new cello concerto, only to humiliate him at rehearsal. It's a diabolical scheme to force her back into his keeping. If she doesn't comply he will devastate her husband by informing him of their past relationship. So she shoots him.

Bette Davis would go to extreme lengths to safeguard her wholesome screen image. Off the rails she may have slipped from time to time as a story character but never while the cameras were rolling.

Such delicacy seems to have been adopted as a general studio rule for the duration of the Second World War. Nobody is actually on record as confirming a tacitly agreed ban on mistress characters but a graph of their pre-

sence and activity in screenplays would show a spectacular plunge from a peak in the 'thirties to a zero during the first half of the 'forties. Infidelity was not good for the morale of the fighting forces, male or female.

Morals were a different matter. It was a fine distinction which, in essence, came down to a case of lust or, at best, forbidden love out, romance in.

Quickie on-leave romance was permissible with or without the sanctity of marriage; after all, practically everybody was doing it . . . but not with a mistress and most definitely *not*, in the case of the girls they left behind, with a lover, unless she truly believed herself to be a war widow. Affairs had to be on a one-to-one basis. Otherwise the demoralizing effect on men and women separated from their loved ones and far from home could have been calamitous.

It was not until two years after the end of the war, allowing time for the studios to re-tool their story and production departments, that the self-imposed ban was seen to have been lifted.

A spate of movies involving adultery or third

Wartime morality was on trial when Lew Ayres and Ann Sheridan faced each other across the courtroom in The Unfaithful *(opposite).*

Tragedy engulfed small-town doctor Paul Muni and his unbending wife Flora Robson when he sought affection from a younger woman in We Are Not Alone *(below).*

parties suddenly began to appear in 1947. There may have been unintentional significance in the fact that the first of them was bluntly called *The Unfaithful* (1947) and was a loose re-working of *The Letter*, one of the last films involving marital infidelity to be shown before wartime self-censorship (both films were from the same studios, Warner Brothers).

The admirable but under-used Ann Sheridan made a bold bid in this and its contemporary *Nora Prentiss* (1947) to take over the mantle of the screen's top 'other woman'.

The Unfaithful faced up to the very problem women's pictures had sought studiously to avoid during the war years. Sheridan and

Zachary Scott had married hastily before he was posted overseas. Now, after getting to know each other all over again in the ten months since he was demobilized, they have settled into a secure, serene marriage.

Returning from a friend's party one night while he is out of town on business, she is confronted by an intruder. There is a struggle and she knifes him to death.

It seems a cut-and-dried case of self-defence until the couple's lawyer friend (Lew Ayres) and the police begin catching her out in evasions and half-truths.

It emerges gradually that while the husband was serving in the Pacific loneliness and worry

led her into a casual, meaningless relationship with a sculptor who had sculpted a head of her (the equivalent of the fateful letter device in the Bette Davis film on which the mystery turns). He has been trying to rekindle the affair, and the struggle and accidental killing (not pre-meditated as in *The Letter*) is the tragic result.

Neither as devious nor as morally unfaithful as the Davis character, Sheridan resigns herself with dignity to her trial and the fact that her much-loved husband has lost faith in her. The lawyer who defends her brings the couple together again in a climactic, sensitively written homily reminding each of them of the pressures the other was under during their separation and pointing out the futility of wrecking a solid, loving marriage by opting too hastily for divorce.

David Goodis, posthumously noted these days as an author of hard-boiled crime fiction in the Raymond Chandler mould, wrote an intelligent, suspenseful screenplay, the only one he would ever own to during his unhappy spell as a Hollywood scriptwriter.

An introductory voice-over says, 'The problem with which it deals . . . is of our time', and *The Unfaithful* certainly seemed to touch a responsive nerve. With Ann Sheridan's impressive performance and the movie's topical relevance it was a popular hit.

So was *Nora Prentiss*, an outright weepie in which a doctor (Kent Smith), desperate to keep his affair with Sheridan's nightclub singer from his wife, runs foul of the law and ruins his own life.

Major women stars were ready and eager to ride that first post-war wave of adulterous love.

Joan Crawford ventured down a Back Street of sorts as *Daisy Kenyon* (1947). She is the long-term mistress of lawyer Dana Andrews, a selfish type who refuses to divorce his wife (Ruth Warrick).

Finally giving up on him, Daisy settles for the less demanding love of Henry Fonda and marries him, whereupon her ex-lover is galvanized into getting a divorce and tries to subvert the marriage.

Romance was not Henry Fonda's métier. He was, by his own admission, suitably cast as 'the less demanding' lover. He wrote in his autobiography:

Love scenes are difficult for me, not just because they're in front of a camera. I've never felt like a terrific lover on screen or in private. Sure I had to kiss girls in pictures, Bette Davis, Barbara Stanwyck, Joan Crawford, Joan Bennett, but I wasn't any good at it.

He was married five times!

Lana Turner, meanwhile, was reaping some of her best notices to date for deceiving her considerably older husband, Spencer Tracy, in *Cass Timberlane* (1947).

Adapted from a Sinclair Lewis best-seller, it cast her as a high-spirited girl from the wrong side of the tracks whose marriage to Tracy's set-in-his-ways judge earns the disapproval of his small-town social set.

Bored with her life and his friends, she takes up with the local playboy (Zachary Scott) and is injured when his car crashes on one of their illicit trysts.

The accident jolts her back to her senses,

making her realize there is no love like a steadfast, if dull, love.

Audiences said 'amen' to that and *Cass Timberlane* still rates a place in *Variety*'s list of all-time top money-making movies.

By the end of 1947, then, extra-marital affairs were very much back in business. But something of the spice was going out of them.

Moral codes had been upturned by the war and society's more open tolerance of sexual indiscretion. As Lana Turner herself comments in her autobiography: 'In any love story made then, the challenge was to suggest the passion that the censors kept off the screen.'

With times and attitudes changing so rapidly, particularly under the growing influence of French and Italian movies which were more outspoken than the English-language studios had ever dared to be, the censor increasingly found himself fighting a rearguard action. Infidelity no longer had the novelty or the allure of the forbidden. The quasi-romantic appeal of the eternal triangle began to ebb away.

Few melodramas in the old, well-tried mould followed that Indian summer of 1947. An adaptation of Flaubert's classic of adultery *Madame Bovary* (1949), with Jennifer Jones, married to Van Heflin, committing it with Louis Jourdan, failed to rekindle the public's interest in the subject.

Even star names were no longer the collateral they had once been. *East Side, West Side* (1949) furnished James Mason, newly emigrated to Hollywood, with Barbara Stanwyck for a wife and Ava Gardner for a mistress. But the triangle failed to fall into place as far as the paying public was concerned.

This movie, all but forgotten, at least has the distinction of adding a small romantic footnote to future history books. Billed sixth in the cast was an aspiring actress in only her third film who would years later win super-stardom in a sphere nobody could have foreseen at that time. The film's director Mervyn LeRoy chanced one day to introduce Nancy Davis to Ronald Reagan.

LeRoy was coming to the conclusion, even as he worked on *East Side, West Side*, that its type of theme was on the way out. He wrote in his autobiography, *Take One*:

The whole business was changing. Television was the vehicle of that change . . . One of the major changes, I felt, was that certain types of movie would soon become a thing of the past. Television would do the types of programmes it could do best and cheapest, programmes that required little outdoor action, no vast sweeps of sets. They would stick pretty much to intimate things.

. . . As the women's picture had traditionally done.

That *East Side, West Side*, with all the lineage and production values that had hall-marked the past popularity of its kind — best-selling novel, major stars with guaranteed box-office pull, a story ambience of money, power and sophistication — should fail to click was the writing on the wall.

The women's picture would thrive for a few more years and enjoy a brief renaissance under Ross Hunter.

But as one of its symbols and talismens the kept woman effectively became a fallen woman.

4

The Girls They Left Behind

WOMEN AND WAR DON'T MIX. It has always been a cardinal rule of movies that women, on aggregate the deciding factor in the choice of film when a couple opt to see one, baulked at the very thought of war. A war film is, by definition, a man's film.

Yet perversely warfare has been the trigger-point for more women's pictures than any other subject, situation or theme serving as a source for emotion.

Inevitably so. In a century of war, few have not been personally touched by it. Drama and tragedy have rippled out of warfare into the consciousness of all, if only at second or third hand.

Remove the noise and horror of battle and what remains are the most powerful elements for emotional conflict experienced by twentieth-century man or woman — the forcible parting of loved ones, danger, death, affliction, tragedy, the anguish of uncertainty, the heightened, heady intoxication of a fleeting romance.

One movie above all others is inseparable from the lore of the Second World War. *Mrs Miniver* (1942) is a women's picture in every frame, from its opening shot of Greer Garson eyeing a frivolous, wildly expensive hat in a shop window and debating whether she can afford it. It was a shrewd bait, calculated to hook every woman watching it.

This study of an allegedly typical British middle-class family in wartime was more than a movie; it was a secret weapon, propaganda for a beleaguered Britain whose emotional impact

Gary Cooper and Helen Hayes in A Farewell to Arms *(opposite).*

on neutral America was worth, Churchill estimated at the time, a dozen battleships.

Pauline Kael, with characteristic wise-after-the-event hindsight, has described it as 'this generally offensive picture', and, in turn, comes close to being gratuitously offensive herself to the millions on both sides of the Atlantic who welcomed and applauded it.

True, much of *Mrs Miniver* can be seen as ludicrous — the standard of living which represented England as a never-never-land of ease and affluence, the almost Victorian class-consciousness which tied the nobility and the artisan class into the central story-line in a rigidly measured pecking order, the too-facile dosages of heroism and romance and tragedy.

But it was a film of its time. It wrung people's hearts even as it uplifted them. It was, particularly for women flattered into recognizing a measure of Mrs Miniver's gallantry and fortitude in themselves, a skilled exercise in audience identification, even if its own identity was marginally false.

The film scooped the Oscar pool that year ('one of the most scandalously smug of all Academy Award winners' — Miss Kael again), with Greer Garson for Best Actress, William Wyler for Director, Teresa Wright for Supporting Actress, three technical awards and, crowning all, the trophy for Best Picture. *Mrs Miniver* remains to this day one of only two outright women's pictures (with *Rebecca*) to win that coveted title.

The film ushered in the era of wartime women's pictures which would flourish for the

next ten years, well past the actual end of hostilities. Even so, it was not exactly a novelty.

Silent films throughout the 'twenties and talkies into the middle of the 'thirties had found ready audiences, and not a little critical favour, for emotional dramas deriving from First World War themes.

George Cukor, the great 'women's director', had served his apprenticeship on *The Virtuous Sin* (1930), his second assignment as a co-director. This was a movie which established Kay Francis as a star, launching her on her long series of romantic roles, in this case giving herself to a general (Walter Huston) as a desperate last resort to save her husband, a bacteriologist, from a front-line death sentence. Kenneth McKenna, who played the husband and was later to turn director, married her the following year.

The finest of these early war weepies, probably also the least true to its origins, was *A Farewell to Arms* (1932), the first of Ernest Hemingway's novels to be filmed.

The book's enduring power lies in its depiction of the horrors of warfare. But it was the idyllic, ill-fated love story the author had woven through them which took precedence in the screenplay.

Gary Cooper and Helen Hayes played the army lieutenant and the English nurse who fall in love while he is on leave from the front and are subsequently reunited when he is wounded.

Parted once more, their love, and correspondence, are thwarted by a jealous major and only after desperately tracing her through the chaos of the war zone does the lieutenant reach her side again, just in time to exchange vows of eternal love before she dies after giving birth to their stillborn child.

The noise of battle was not entirely eliminated but, in the interests of the women's market the movie so successfully catered to, it was subdued.

The performances of both stars were generally acclaimed and the film was nominated for four Academy Awards, including Best Picture.

Only one person seemed displeased with the results — Hemingway himself. In typical Hollywood fashion, two alternative endings had been shot, one according to the book, the other happier, according to the commercial rules. It was the latter the public saw on the film's

THE GIRLS THEY LEFT BEHIND

A hymn to the fortitude of British womanhood in the Second World War – Walter Pidgeon, Greer Garson and Henry Wilcoxson in Mrs Miniver.

initial release (the nurse lived) and the author complained: 'I did not intend a happy ending.'

A Farewell to Arms has been remade twice. Thinly disguised but unmistakably Hemingway, even though his name was not credited, *Force of Arms* (1951) updated the story to the Second World War and teamed William Holden as a battle-shocked GI and Nancy Olson as the nurse.

David O. Selznick sought to do belated justice by Hemingway with his massively overblown *A Farewell to Arms* (1957). Spectacle was in vogue and no expense was spared to restore the novel's scenes of battle to their proper perspective in the story. It was a disastrous decision. The threading love story, so delicately spun in the 1932 version, was doomed to be swamped by the logistics of a $4

million production even it if had not been acted out so stiltedly by Rock Hudson and Selznick's wife Jennifer Jones.

Audiences bypassed it and its financial losses brought Selznick's distinguished movie reign to an ignominious end. The man responsible for such classics as *Gone with the Wind, Rebecca, Spellbound, Duel in the Sun* and dozens more never again produced a movie.

The Fountain (1935) lived up to its moisturizing imagery of title as a tear-jerker but, with the best of intentions, compromised its potential by also endeavouring to live up to its origins.

Charles Morgan's heavy-going novel, a literary *succès d'estime*, examined the cruelty and futility of war through the personalized prism of a three-way love story.

Ann Harding is an Englishwoman married to a German officer, Paul Lukas, during the First World War and living in Holland. Among the captured British officers brought to a nearby fort for internment is Brian Aherne, whose pupil she had once been back in England before marriage. They meet again and fall in love.

Her husband returns wounded and she nurses him devotedly but not, he begins to realize, out of love. Like the true officer and gentleman he is, he bows to the inevitable and relinquishes her.

'A beautifully contemplative novel is made into a film exquisite to look at but moving with measured tread,' according to one review.

The public tended to agree and stayed away, though now the film can be better appreciated for the delicacy of its direction by John Cromwell and its thoughtful performances.

There were parallels the same year between *The Fountain* and *The Dark Angel* (1935), a title which still stands as a brand-name for this kind of movie, the wash of tears in the context of war, although the film itself has dated.

Romantic triangles for Paul Lukas and Ann Harding in The Fountain *(below), and for Fredric March, Herbert Marshall and Merle Oberon in* The Dark Angel *(opposite), both dramas set in the First World War.*

Samuel Goldwyn, an expert in sincere emotionalism, remade a silent of ten years earlier about three childhood friends, Kitty, Alan and Gerald. Both men, serving in the same regiment, love Kitty but she favours Alan with a snatched night of love on the eve of embarkation for the front line.

Gerald takes her rejection of him in good part until he learns of the stolen night. He judges Alan to have betrayed the girl and, as the superior officer, sends him on a hazardous mission from which he fails to return.

F-34

Back in England Kitty, still loving Alan but believing him to be dead, agrees to marry Gerald. Alan, however, has survived, wounded and blinded, and through a mutual friend the three are reunited.

Alan, not wanting pity or to disrupt the marriage plans of the other two, memorizes every detail of the room in which they are to meet so that he can conceal his blindness from them. At first they are deceived but true love is all-seeing, and Kitty, realizing the truth, pledges herself to him.

The Dark Angel, handsomely produced, seems over-mannered nowadays but its skilfully wrought tenderness still has the power to move. The playwright Lillian Hellman was one of the co-authors of the screenplay.

The film transformed Merle Oberon into an international star with her second Hollywood role.

Years later she would always claim that the earlier silent version had been her favourite film as a child and had inspired her to make a career in movies.

THE GIRLS THEY LEFT BEHIND

War clouds shadowed the love
affairs of Joan Fontaine and
Tyrone Power in This Above All
(right) and Vivien Leigh and
Robert Taylor in Waterloo Bridge
(opposite).

According to *Merle*, the biography by Charles Higham and Roy Molesey, the star's on-screen romancing dilemma in *The Dark Angel* was being duplicated off the set, if not with quite the same degree of etherealism.

When production started she had just ended an intense affair with Leslie Howard and was simultaneously making passes (rejected in the event) at Gary Cooper!

Of the film the London *Times* declared:

[It] makes a systematic and often very skilful appeal to those untrustworthy emotions which may suddenly cause the most hardened intellects to dissolve before the most obvious sentimentality.

Miss Oberon's performance, along with those of Fredric March (Alan) and Herbert Marshall (Gerald) spurred critics to superlatives for its quality of 'restraint' and 'sympathetic understanding'.

There was to be one final backward glance to the emotionalism of the First World War before an even greater one engulfed the world and the theme of war-generated romance began to lose its vicariously safe, at-a-remove appeal.

Waterloo Bridge (1940) went into production in 1939 even as Hitler was invading Poland. It had its New York première on 14 May 1940, the day Nazi bombers obliterated Rotterdam.

For the next two years until 1942, when the world had learned to adjust itself to war conditions, the subject was to be strictly avoided in women's pictures. It was probably no coincidence, either, that its reinstatement as an acceptable thematic background coincided

with America's own entry into the war at the end of 1941.

Waterloo Bridge had first been filmed in 1931 with Mae Clark and Kent Douglass (who later renamed himself Douglass Montgomery). Now the roles of the tragic ballerina and the British army officer torn apart by war went to Vivien Leigh in her first movie since *Gone with the Wind* (she would have preferred to play opposite Laurence Olivier in *Pride and Prejudice*) and Robert Taylor.

They meet by chance in a fog on Waterloo Bridge during the First World War, fall wildly in love and attempt to marry before he has to

leave for the front. Red tape thwarts them and the dancer misses a performance to see him off at Waterloo Station.

She is fired from the ballet company for her non-appearance and, unable to find work, sinks deeper into poverty. Her will to survive disintegrates when she reads that her lover is believed missing or killed and under force of circumstance turns to prostitution.

While she is touting for business one night at Waterloo Station she sees him. Their passionate reunion is shadowed by her secret shame and the fear that he will discover how she is living. He takes her home for a few snatched hours of happiness but her guilt causes her to confess to his mother and she walks quietly out

of his life. As he is frantically trying to find her, she throws herself under a lorry on Waterloo Bridge.

A definitive weepie, still potent in its aura of romantic tragedy, it is lyrically directed by Mervyn LeRoy and played like a rhapsody by its two stars, with immaculate support from denizens of Hollywood's British colony.

A prologue and epilogue were added to the original screenplay to provide an eloquent link between the two world wars and tune the story to its contemporary times. An ageing, grey-haired Robert Taylor, back in uniform for the modern war, pauses on the bridge and gazes into the Thames, remembering with sadness the last one . . .

It marked the first appearance of the Taylor moustache, to become his trademark — cultivated for the film on the grounds that it was the custom for British army officers in the 1914-18 war to wear one.

Taylor always cited *Waterloo Bridge* as his favourite movie.

Hollywood, from then on, concentrated its war effort on adventure, thrills, action or the occasional anti-Nazi drama, boosting the morale and fighting spirit of the men in the front line or underlining the noble cause for which they and their loved ones back home were making sacrifices.

The first two movies to show that this was as much a woman's war as a man's, *Mrs Miniver* and *This Above All* (1942), both focused on the Britain-at-bay period of 1940 between Dunkirk and the Blitz. Could it have been entirely coincidental that both films were unleashed on an American public being newly called to arms during the same May week?

The realities of war are grimly brought home into the Minivers' secure backyard when Clem Miniver (Walter Pidgeon) answers the appeal for 'little ships' by adding his river cruiser to the Dunkirk armada.

So that nobody, especially neutral (at the time of production) Americans, can be left in any doubt that Britain's crisis at that historic moment was no less fraught with peril for the nation's womanhood, Mrs Miniver, while her husband is away on his secret mission, stumbles on a downed Nazi flyer hiding in her garden and faces up to the challenge of a gun-toting fanatical enemy with a gallantry quite the equal of her husband's.

Later their house is artistically damaged by German bombs and their daughter-in-law (Teresa Wright) is killed by gunfire from a strafing German plane during an air-raid. Such neat, tacit salutes to the women's audience were craftily built into the plot, acknowledging that women, too, were fighting the good fight and dying for the cause — the girl's young Miniver husband is an RAF pilot helping to wage the Battle of Britain, which he survives unscathed.

This Above All, based on a novel (by Eric Knight who, at the furthermost extreme, had written *Lassie Come Home*) with more serious intent than Hollywood in those days judged was commercially acceptable for a screenplay, took Dunkirk as its starting-point.

Tyrone Power, then at his peak as a matinée idol, was daringly cast against type as a radically minded working-class British soldier, traumatized by his experiences during the Dunkirk evacuation, who deserts on the principle that an England ruled by the upper classes is not worth fighting for.

He is taken in hand by Joan Fontaine, a serving aircraftswoman from the aristocracy he so despises, who falls in love with him and coaxes him round to the ideal of patriotism.

Comes the Blitz in London to serve as a timely catalyst for the doubter's disaffection from King and country. He redeems himself with an act of heroism during an air-raid which clears him of the taint of cowardice and assures him of the love of a good woman, albeit a high-born one.

As in so many films of its time the pertinent social realism of the original novel was discreetly veiled by an unquestioning, anodyne romanticism. But, taken on the terms it had opted for as a commercial product, it was effective and successful at the box office.

'Its strength and disarming distinction', according to the New York Times, 'is that it tells a very moving love story with a sensitive regard for tensile passions against a background of England at war.'

Indeed, England at war inspired a speech from Joan Fontaine's character, explaining what the peril facing her beloved country meant to her, which was positively Churchillian in its rhetorical power to move anyone who heard it.

This Above All still exhibits a superiority over the more celebrated Mrs Miniver in one respect — its Hollywoodian picture of England and the English in that finest hour suggested a more heightened mood of realism and truth. Its art design and sets, in fact, won Academy Awards and its cinematography merited a nomination.

As though to drive home to American women the sacrifices their British sisters were making, The War Against Mrs Hadley (1942) was a curious but effective item of propaganda masquerading as a women's picture.

A selfish Washington socialite played by Fay Bainter, one of the cinema's most reliable and recognizable supporting actresses in a rare leading role, refuses to trim her extravagant life-style to the bleak winds of the war effort and its restrictions. Mrs Hadley was the antithesis of Mrs Miniver! Eventually, of course, she sees the error of her unpatriotic ways and did sterling duty in rallying indignant audi-

ences — and they were large ones for this hit — round the flag.

Miss Bainter turned up around the same time in Journey for Margaret (1942), though heavily overshadowed by its unknown titular star, the soon-to-be queen of moppets Margaret O'Brien.

This was unashamed weepie territory, based on a documentary book about a 5-year-old orphan of the London Blitz adopted and taken across the Atlantic by an American newspaperman (Robert Young) to face the emotional pains of adjusting to a new mother (Laraine Day) and a new life.

America and Hollywood were by now themselves adjusting to the realities of a war which, for them, had effectively begun a few months earlier with the attack on Pearl Harbor.

While Clark Gable was working with Lana Turner on Somewhere I'll Find You (1942) his wife Carole Lombard was killed in an air crash on her way home from a war-bond selling tour.

Miss Turner wrote in her memoirs: 'The whole studio was in a state of shock. A pall settled over everyone connected with the picture.' Her own sense of shock might have been intensified by a rumour that Carole Lombard, scheduled to travel by train, had decided to take the plane instead because of 'her uneasiness over my working with Clark'.

Production was halted and for a time came close to being abandoned as Clark Gable grieved inconsolably. But eventually it was completed.

Both stars played war correspondents chasing news and each other in bouts of torrid lovemaking between periods of battle fatigue. The film was not the most distinguished either

Ginger Rogers (opposite) coaxed audiences' tears when she played a prisoner on parole in I'll Be Seeing You.

of them ever made — a bonanza at the box-office nevertheless — but it rates a footnote in the history of wartime Hollywood for a couple of reasons.

MGM got considerable publicity mileage out of Lana Turner's new hairstyle, cut into a short bob and named 'the Victory Hairdo'.

This, according to the publicists, was a conscious, if unlikely, gesture to the efficiency and safety of war work, into which millions of women on both sides of the Atlantic were suddenly finding themselves drafted.

Adopt this style and hair won't get caught in factory machinery, the message ran.

So successful was the gimmick that MGM received a request from British Government sources for detailed instructions on the style and cut to be distributed among women at the work-benches of Britain. If nothing else, it blew an MGM raspberry at rival studio Paramount, then basking in the publicity fame of Veronica Lake's long, peek-a-boo tresses.

After completing *Somewhere I'll Find You*, Clark Gable provided its other historic footnote by enlisting in the US Army Air Corps, swelling the ranks of Hollywood's romantic leading men going off to war.

Invention being the mother (or, in this case, father) of necessity, a new generation of male stars had to be reared quickly to fill the void and one of the most successful of them was to be found somewhere in *Somewhere I'll Find You*, though you had to search hard for Van Johnson's bit part.

The sizzling Gable-Turner teaming would, incidentally, come full circle six years later with the shrewdly titled *Homecoming* (1948), in which, as surgeon and nurse, they indulge in an illicit battlefront romance while his wife Anne Baxter keeps the home fires burning.

Of the new leading men conscripted to hold the studio fort during the enforced absence of the veterans, none rendered more meritorious service to the women's picture than Joseph Cotten.

Youth was not on his side but image was. His strong but kindly features, caring eyes and authoritative yet sensitive voice and speech made him the ideal of every woman's dream of romance. They were, too, qualities which endowed him with a versatility of range, equally at ease in westerns and thrillers, though not noticeably comedies.

A protégé of Orson Welles, Cotten had come to the fore in *Citizen Kane* and two well-regarded thrillers, *Journey into Fear* and Hitchcock's *Shadow of a Doubt*.

His romantic potential first emerged opposite the then 22-year-old Deanna Durbin in *Hers to Hold* (1943), in a teaming which epitomized the opportunities opened up for the likes of him by the departure of the established male stars into the armed forces.

He was 20 years older than his co-star, an age differential which was to become fairly common during these years as story-lines were discreetly adjusted to camouflage the problem of younger actors having gone to serve their country (Greer Garson and Ronald Colman in *Random Harvest*; Joan Fontaine and Charles Boyer in *The Constant Nymph*; Ingrid Bergman with Boyer and Cotten in *Gaslight*; Bette

Ginger Rogers

Davis and Claude Rains in *Mr Skeffington* and *Deception*).

Hers to Hold patriotically contrived to bestride both war-fronts — home and active service — with Miss Durbin, who had recently negotiated the tricky transition from adolescence to womanhood, playing a war-worker who takes a job in an aircraft factory (though neglecting to adopt the Victory Hairdo) so that she can be near the flyer she loves. Eyes commenced to dampen when her hero flew off into the wild blue yonder.

Mr Cotten himself took off the following year with four unabashed women's pictures, three of which put him in uniform (the odd one out was *Gaslight*, in which he saved Ingrid Bergman from the evil intent of Charles Boyer).

One of them was *Since You Went Away* (1944), a near three-hour saga viewed by some as the *Mrs Miniver* of wartime American womanhood.

Epic in all respects except that of its low-key, improbably soft-focus picture of a 'typical' well-heeled middle-class family, particularly the womenfolk, it paraded a regiment of top-brass stars, Claudette Colbert, Jennifer Jones, a newly grown-up Shirley Temple, Agnes Moorehead, Monty Woolley, Lionel Barrymore and many other worthy, if less heady, names.

Among them was Robert Walker, a young actor beginning to gain recognition.

Five years earlier he and Jennifer Jones, then unknown, had married. Miss Jones, discovered by David Selznick, struck stardom gold spectacularly with her first major role in *The Song of Bernadette*, winning the 1943 Best Actress Oscar. *Since You Went Away* was her follow-up movie, carefully tailored for her by Selznick.

By now Hollywood gossip was linking their names romantically and the Jones-Walker marriage had broken up. Nevertheless Selznick wanted Robert Walker for *Since You Went*

The woes of war enhanced the prestige and popularity of Jennifer Jones.

Away and borrowed him from MGM to co-star with his estranged wife, the only time they ever appeared together.

They subsequently divorced and Selznick and Jones were married. Walker, it was generally believed, never got over it. Plagued by emotional problems, he would fritter away a career which promised to develop into one of Hollywood's finest, temporarily recovering his equilibrium for one final and unforgettable performance in Hitchcock's *Strangers on a Train*.

Within months of completing it he was dead from an overdose of sedatives.

Since You Went Away was looked at askance by many contemporary critics wary of its idealized American home-and-beauty view of the war's impact on a family almost too goody-goody to be true, and its glossy production values. But these were the very elements which made it a massive hit with the public. Nowadays, with *The Best Years of Our Lives*, it is rated as the quintessential classic, albeit a flawed one, of Hollywood home-front escapism during those grim years.

One of its by-products was a steady and popular on-screen romantic partnership between Jennifer Jones and Joseph Cotten.

Before it was to resume, however, he was to be found romancing Ginger Rogers in *I'll Be Seeing You* (1944), a curiosity for those times in both its story and its appeal.

Shirley Temple was also carried over from *Since You Went Away* into this downbeat sentimental Selznick drama, as was the 'family' texture.

Ginger Rogers plays a woman returning home on weekend parole from prison, where she is serving a sentence for manslaughter. On the train she meets Cotten's shell-shocked Army sergeant just released from a mental hospital. She takes him home to her family and over the weekend a wispy, cautious romance begins to grow out of their mutual sense of being outcasts.

Both performers were deemed 'excellent' by the *New York Times*, Cotten playing 'with supreme restraint and with a calm and determined independence that beautifully reveals his pain and pride' and Miss Rogers proving herself 'altogether moving as the girl likewise injured by fate'.

Cotten and Jennifer Jones were reunited in his next project, *Love Letters* (1945), scarcely less of a story oddity than *I'll Be Seeing You*.

The setting this time is England, and Cotten is a British officer at the front persuaded, against his better judgement, to 'ghost'-write literate love letters for a devil-may-care comrade-in-arms to send back home to his fiancée.

Later, injured and repatriated home to convalesce, he is unsuspectingly brought face to face with the girl, who doesn't know of his existence, through a sequence of coincidences and shared acquaintances.

She is suffering from amnesia; a fey, will-o'-the-wispish beauty with a dark mystery shadowing her past. Cotten, secretly in love with her himself since the days he read and answered her letters as proxy ('a pin-up girl of the spirit' is how he explains his obsession with her), probes into her background. He discovers she has served a prison sentence for stabbing his erstwhile comrade to death after

their marriage. The key to the tragedy was the *ersatz* love letters to her.

It's a wholly implausible film, yet intriguing; a lyrical romance with grafts of gothic mystery in which coincidence is writ outrageously large. Fortuitously, Cotten inherits his aunt's house deep in the Essex marshes which as luck, or, at any rate, a screen-writer, would have it, turns out to be only a mile or so from the scene of the girl's crime.

Love Letters affords a minor insight into the cosmetic treatment often judged necessary to render a story palatable for screen purposes. In Chris Massie's original novel *Pity My Simpliciy* (the movie updated it from the First to the Second World War) the Cotten character is called Maurice . . . not a fashionably romantic name. There is a subsidiary character, a brother called Alan. For the film the brother is omitted from the story and Maurice is re-named Alan.

Even more potent was the merchandizing of the film's theme music as a hit-parade song with added lyrics. It became enormously popular — a standard even now — and marked out *Love Letters* as one of the earliest movies to capitalize on the publicity value of extending its title to a pop song. It was the reverse process of *I'll Be Seeing You*, which borrowed its title and soundtrack themes from the famous song.

Certainly the simplest and probably the most affecting of the soldier boy-meets-girl-only-to-part romances around this time was *The Clock* (1945; UK title *Under the Clock*) which gave Judy Garland the first non-singing role of her career, following immediately on the phenomenal success of *Meet Me in St Louis*.

Even its genesis was simple. 'I produced *The Clock* to give Judy a kick. She wanted to do a straight picture,' producer Arthur Freed was to recall later.

To direct he brought in Vincente Minnelli and romance was in the air. 'It had begun with *Meet Me in St Louis*,' Arthur Freed said, 'but the real thing happened during the filming of *The Clock*.'

In June 1945, just after the film's New York première, Garland and Minnelli were married. Nine months later a future star was born — Liza Minnelli.

True to Freed's intentions, simplicity is the quality, compounded by the sincerity of its two star performances, which makes *The Clock* such a durable romantic trifle.

Soldier bumps into girl at New York's Penn Station and gallantly helps her out when one of her high heels snaps in the collision. He is on a

THE GIRLS THEY LEFT BEHIND

*Judy Garland (opposite) first
revealed her dramatic capabilities
in* The Clock, *co-starring with
Robert Walker.*

Judy Garland's dramatic capabilities were a revelation for the time, though it would be another ten years before she was called on to exercise them again in *A Star is Born* and a further seven after that until her next non-singing straight-acting cameo in *Judgement at Nuremberg*. Both performances were to win her Academy Award nominations.

The part of the young soldier went to Robert Walker, already sliding into alcoholism following the break-up with Jennifer Jones. It caused production problems and delays.

Judy, herself no stranger to the pressures and curatives of such a situation, took him under her wing. In the early flush of her own romance with the movie's director, she nursed Walker through their scenes together with every consideration and understanding, even searching bars one night after the day's work was over and smuggling him home to dry out so that he would be back in shape for the morrow's shooting.

The Clock struck only just in time with its theme, overworked by now but never quite so refreshingly, of 'crowding a lifetime of happiness into a few fleeting hours'. Less than two months after its US release the war in Europe ended; the cause for snatching at happiness was all but removed.

A new emotional problem, a new theme, superseded it: the difficulties of readjustment for the men returning home and the wives and families they returned to.

The Best Years of Our Lives (1946) is a monument to that period. It remains one of the great movies of all time.

weekend pass, a stranger to the city, diffident and inexperienced with women.

She, taking pity on him and at a loose end, volunteers to show him the town.

As the hours tick by they are tentatively drawn into a chaste love-affair. They separate, arranging to meet again for the evening, miss each other and, as they search the town, independently realize their true feelings for each other. Reunited, they brave the harassing bureaucracy of marrying in a hurry before the Penn Station clock strikes the witching hour which marks the end of his leave.

The *New York Times* capsuled it thus:

... the kind of picture that leaves one with a warm feeling toward his fellow-man, especially towards the young folks who today are trying to crowd a lifetime of happiness into a few fleeting hours.

THE GIRLS THEY LEFT BEHIND

'*Soldiers from the wars returning*' was the theme which inspired one of the screen masterpieces of the 'forties, The Best Years of Our Lives. Opposite: (top left) Harold Russell (Homer), Dana Andrews (Fred) and Fredric March (Al) meet on the plane taking them home to Boone City; (top right) Al has trouble re-adjusting to the old routine, while (lower right) Fred faces trouble with his good-time wife Marie (Virginia Mayo).

No idealized tushery, this, but a reflection of its times so scrupulously observed and truthful that millions identified with its fiction.

From the start its provenance was distinguished. Samuel Goldwyn originated the idea after reading a news item about a war veteran's readjustment to civilian life. He commissioned novelist McKinlay Kantor to prepare a treatment (published as a novel in blank verse *Glory for Me*) and playwright Robert E. Sherwood, one of the great contemporary names of American theatre, to write the screenplay.

For his cast he assembled Fredric March, Myrna Loy, Dana Andrews, Teresa Wright, Virginia Mayo, Cathy O'Donnell and a genuine war hero, the non-actor Harold Russell, who had lost both hands in a grenade explosion.

This proved a masterstroke. Russell's heart-rending performance won him the Academy Award for Best Supporting Actor, plus a second Oscar 'for bringing hope and courage to his fellow veterans'. It is the only time in Academy Award history that an actor has won two Oscars for the same role. Russell never repeated his acting experience. He became a businessman far removed from Hollywood.

The universality of its theme made *The Best Years of Our Lives* a film for everyman rather than a women's picture. But the elements threaded through it in a story weave of three homecoming servicemen and the reactions of their womenfolk and families to these 'strangers' were those which had long governed the female market and the movie found particular favour among women.

It won a clutch of Oscars including Best Actor (Fredric March), Best Director (William Wyler), Best Screenplay (Robert Sherwood), Best Music (Hugo Friedhofer) and, to top them all, Best Picture.

And it set a trend. Clone movies proliferated for the next two or three years, but none that matched its standards.

One of the better examples was *From This Day Forward* (1946), which broadened its narrative scope by flashbacking to pre-war days as a counterpoint to the harsh economic and emotional realities faced by returning war hero Mark Stevens and his wife Joan Fontaine.

Jane Russell was — improbably to filmgoers of that period — the heroine of *Young Widow* (1946) in her second role after her sensational bosom-heaving, censor-baiting début in *The Outlaw*. This time a woman's post-war adjustment was the focus — to the memory of her love for a husband who has been killed in action. It was awash with tears, as was the most lookalike of all *The Best Years of Our Lives* copies, *Till the End of Time* (1946), in which three servicemen settled back into peacetime routines, including one who had lost both legs. Dorothy McGuire was the principal star.

103

THE GIRLS THEY LEFT BEHIND

Edward Dmytryk, one of Hollywood's most stylish and incisive directors, turned the familiar story-line into compelling drama, a worthy successor to its distinguished forerunner.

Till the End of Time merits at least one small niche in any movie hall of fame for registering Robert Mitchum's stake to a star career after a string of B-picture bit parts and a wartime spell in the armed forces (he had come up on the inside track the previous year by securing a surprise Oscar nomination for Best Supporting Actor in *The Story of GI Joe*).

Hollywood imported one of Britain's then favourite screen actresses, Phyllis Calvert, and director Compton Bennett, who had just impressed American producers with his phenomenally successful *The Seventh Veil*, for *My Own True Love* (1948). Melvyn Douglas returns home from the wars to find himself competing with his own son for Miss Calvert's favours. The film, however, did not find much favour with the public.

One quirky variation on the homecoming theme was the awkward situation which could arise when a husband, listed as killed in action, inconveniently turns up at war's end to find his 'widow' committed to another man.

It was a dilemma which confronted Robert Mitchum and Greer Garson in *Desire Me* (1947), a remake of a 1925 silent called *The Homecoming*.

To add insult to the injury, Mitchum's soldier returning from the dead has been replaced in his wife's affections by his former comrade-in-arms (Richard Hart).

The film, a disaster by most standards, has its shame attested by an ignominious footnote in cinema history.

George Cukor directed it 'from a script that didn't really make sense', but, a troubled production from the start, it was largely re-shot by Mervyn LeRoy: 'A rotten script, a script that made absolutely no sense.' Two of Hollywood's

Tough-guy-to-be Robert Mitchum served his apprenticeship for stardom in the unashamed tear-jerker Till the End of Time.

ace directors . . . but the result was still, in LeRoy's words, a 'botch'. Both men insisted that their names didn't appear on the credits and it remains the only film ever released without a director's credit.

Now that peace was securely established, memories of war were fast dimming as the 'forties came to an end and it was probably Samuel Goldwyn who delivered the last contemporary insight into the impact the war had had on women and women's pictures; a fitting valedictory from the producer of *The Dark Angel* and *The Best Years of Our Lives*.

Flashbacks bridged the gulf between remembrance of times just past and the realities of the new post-war world in *My Foolish Heart* (1949) as they had linked the two world wars at the beginning of the second in *Waterloo Bridge*.

A sad little short story by J.D. Salinger with the unpromisng title *Uncle Wiggily in Connecticut* inspired this superbly polished exercise in heartache.

Susan Hayward is a woman grappling with a troubled conscience and a drink problem, poised to walk out on her husband and young daughter.

At the height of the war she and a flyer (Dana Andrews) had been passionately in love. He is killed in a plane crash and she is expecting his child. To give it a name she has deliberately seduced the fiancé of her best friend at college into marrying her and let him believe the baby is his.

As a last, cutting blow at the innocent husband whose unhappiness she has caused she intends before leaving to tell him the truth but the old college friend, still loyal to both parties, prevents her. As she listens sympathetically to the poignant memories of the past, her understanding helps to shift the received image of the wife from spiteful shrew to a hapless victim of the war acting out of desperation.

The screenplay was unashamedly emotional, the production unerringly targeted at its female market (the flashback memories are triggered by the wife's re-discovery, as she is packing to walk out on her husband and child, of the old dress she was wearing when she first encountered the flyer at a party). There was even a title song — by 'Love Letters' composer Victor Young — which stayed lodged in the hit parade for months and remains a standard.

My Foolish Heart, thanks to the Goldwyn touch with such subjects, was a winner at the box office. It made a front-rank star of Susan Hayward, of whom *Newsweek* wrote: 'She makes the most of her first chance at an honest, demanding characterization by realizing it with an admirable sincerity and understanding.' For the second time she was nominated for an Academy Award.

In some ways the film is typical of critical attitudes which prevailed towards the women's picture. The *New York Times* non-committally declared:

THE GIRLS THEY LEFT BEHIND

The most durable of all wartime romances was surely that between Humphrey Bogart and Ingrid Bergman in Casablanca *(opposite).*

Every so often there comes a picture which is obviously designed to pull the plugs out of the tear glands and cause the ducts to overflow.

Disapproval is implicit.

Time magazine conceded:

In its dry-eyed moments this damp fable is brightened by some well-written patches of wryly amusing dialogue. The whole picture wears an air of quality thanks to Samuel Goldwyn's handsome production and a group of sincere performances.

Again there appears to be a grudging, if not condescending, surprise that an emotional subject should offer some redeeming production virtues.

Reassessments by critics today tend to allow that *My Foolish Heart* is superior moviemaking irrespective of whatever genre standards it is judged by. Ordinary filmgoers were way ahead of them, endorsing its solid gold box-office value right from the start.

Warfare, or at any rate the emotional wash from it, lost its questionable romanticism and notional appeal with the end of the Second World War. The atomic bomb saw to that. So, too, did movies themselves. The new realism in life and on screen left neither place nor taste for vicarious tear-shedding at the expense of human conflict and heartache.

The Korean War produced one affecting love story — a true one — in *Love is a Many Splendored Thing* (1955). Jennifer Jones, now a veteran of so many wartime anguishes, played a Eurasian doctor in Hong Kong whose ill-starred romance with William Holden's married war correspondent on his leaves from the war zone bore all the classic hallmarks of the genre. As with *Love Letters*, her performance was Oscar-nominated. And the title music yielded an enduring hit song.

Based on Han Suyin's autobiographical novel, it reflected the changing times and more socially aware approach Hollywood was now adopting by introducing a firm sub-theme of both racial prejudice and pride into its romantic idyll.

Han Suyin, half-Chinese and half-Belgian, wrote the story of her love-affair with a British journalist, a correspondent for *The Times*, shortly after he was killed in action. It was a best-seller and so was the movie.

Two years later Hollywood firmly grasped the nettle of inter-racial romance. *Sayonara* (1957), from a book by James A. Michener, examined the topical and still ticklish issue of love and marriage between US servicemen stationed in Japan and local girls.

A literary descendant of *Madam Butterfly*, the story had a racially prejudiced major, Marlon Brando, falling in love with a Japanese actress (Miko Taka). The affair was, of course, doomed, but not the film, sensitively written and directed, which proved to be one of the year's top earners.

Recent movies such as *Coming Home* and *The Deer Hunter* have dealt with the effects of the Vietnam War on the womenfolk who waited back home no less stoically than their mothers and grandmothers had in previous wars. But the macho complexion of cinema in the 1970s ensured they couldn't be mistaken for women's pictures.

106

Romance and war seem an ill mix in the nuclear age and it's probably no coincidence that, with the tentative revival of the women's picture in the 1980s, themes touching on war, such as those embodied in *The Return of the Soldier*, *Another Time*, *Another Place*, *Sophie's Choice* and *Plenty* have looked back to one or other of the century's two great world wars for their catalysts.

They have come, with the mellowing of time, to represent periods with which those enduring human virtues of fortitude, sacrifice, gallantry and high romanticism are now synonymous, not forgetting, either, the potency of nostalgia.

One movie above all others with a wartime theme epitomizes that nostalgia.

Casablanca (1942) transcends the barriers of category; not solely thriller, not entirely romance, hardly an action picture. But stripped down to the axle of its tremulous might-have-been love story between Humphrey Bogart and Ingrid Bergman, its chemistry is overwhelmingly that of the women's picture.

It has the inevitable triangle: Bogart's cynical Rick, Bergman's Ilsa and her freedom-fighter husband Paul Henreid, the emotional currents between them heightened by being channelled into a crucible of fear and threat.

It has the bitter-sweet poignancy of a desperate love-affair which can never find fulfilment and, in the character of Rick, the timeless challenge of the restless buccaneer a woman longs to tame and hold but never will. It even has the element of the husband returned from the dead — Ilsa had embarked on her romance with Rick believing her husband had perished in a concentration camp.

Casablanca is unique in the way it distils quality romanticism, wholly believable, from pulp melodrama.

'Was that cannon fire or is it my heart pounding?' Ilsa wonders aloud during one of her passionate interludes with Rick as the Germans close in on Paris. It's a line which should invite derision; but not as spoken by Bergman in the intoxicating context of her love.

Overlaying the drama and skilfully introduced at crucial moments as a recurring reminder of the poignant romance that might have been is the song 'As Time Goes By', itself a classic of nostalgia.

Even today, it requires only a mention of *Casablanca*'s title or a snatch of the song 'As Time Goes By' to re-kindle a vivid memory or impression of women's pictures in the bleak years of the last world war.

5

The Food of Love

THERE IS SOMETHING about musicians which brings out a sublime movie madness.

Music, Shakespeare claimed, hath charms to soothe the savage breast. Screen-writers knew better. In a scenario music needed to savage breasts before it soothed them.

Or, put another way, Nöel Coward's observation about the potency of cheap music was stood on its head. Music of quality, authentic classical or plastic imitation, was long the favoured instrument for stirring emotions in women's pictures.

Tchaikovsky, Rachmaninov, Grieg, Liszt, Chopin . . . these great masters owe an incalculable debt to the tear-jerker, the weepie, the four-hankie job. Thanks to countless soundtracks their mass appeal spilled out of the concert hall and far beyond the ken of the *cognoscenti*.

Whether or not they would have looked benevolently on the liberties taken with some of their masterpieces is academic.

Some of the most endearing idiocies in movies owe their inspiration to great, or pseudo-great, music.

Long-forgotten and deservedly so, *Concerto* (1946; a.k.a. *I've Always Loved You*) was *fortissimo* musical passion.

Frank Borzage, a veteran director of heartache melodrama, superintended this farrago in the declining years of his career. It chronicles the romantic tormets of a young concert pianist, Catherine McLeod, who falls in love with a great conductor. Despite the beautiful music they make together he holds her at a distance and she marries someone else.

True love eventually finds a way and it leads to the concert hall, where, before an enraptured audience, she is locked in combat with the final movement of a particularly fiendish concerto.

Ingrid Bergman (opposite) made beautiful music in an emotional duet with Leslie Howard for Intermezzo *(left), the film which introduced her to English-speaking audiences.*

THE FOOD OF LOVE

She sees him waiting in the wings. Incandescent, she slowly rises from her stool as the music surges towards its climax, glides past the astonished conductor and throws herself into her long-lost lover's arms, leaving the orchestra to finish the performance as best it can without her ... and, no doubt, leaving her audience fuming with irritation. The more humdrum realities of life, art and professional commitment have no part to play in this kind of script.

Miss McLeod was only doing her duty by it, but it may have been significant that she was relegated to daytime TV soap opera after this, her one and only starring performance.

Movies have always been choosy about the type of musician they spin their dreams around. There has yet to be one, at least with aspirations to romance, which has dealt with the *amours propres* of a bassoonist or a double-bass player.

It's a prejudice which restricts the tonal range of scripts to the keyboard or the stringed instruments, primarily the violin, although there was one notable instance in which the cello was given star billing.

The keyboard is king. Pianists are considered the most romantic of musicians — female pianists in particular. Who, after all, can remain indifferent to the sight and sound of an emotionally overwrought heroine pouring her heart out at the keyboard in cascades of arpeggios or pounding out her frustrations in a fury of chromatic octaves?

Mary Astor was partial to the latter therapy in *The Great Lie* (1941), playing what must be arguably the screen's bitchiest great artist.

No mean pianist herself, she fingered her way through Tchaikovsky's Piano Concerto No. 1, though the soundtrack was dubbed by a professional.

Tchaikovsky was not her only challenge. She was also pitted against Bette Davis in this totally implausible but wildly popular contest between two women for the love of George Brent.

Davis in an unusually quiescent role loves him selflessly, but it is the sophisticated Astor who wins and marries him, more by foul means than fair.

Her self-absorption and pathological pursuit of her celebrity career quickly disillusion him. He goes missing, believed dead, in a plane crash, an inconvenience Astor has barely got over before she is confronted with an even more tiresome one. She is pregnant.

Davis, still carrying her torch sorrowingly, makes a pact with her. As soon as the child is born (it duly is in the wilds of nowhere amid a storm the like of which had hardly been witnessed since Lillian Gish's heyday in silents) Davis takes charge of it, leaving Astor to carry on her affair with Tchaikovsky.

Then Brent returns from the dead. He weighs up the situation, realizes the error of his choice and recognizes the real nature of the viper he married.

The pianist role in *The Great Lie* is one of the showiest on film and won Mary Astor an Academy Award as much, probably, for her theatricals at the keyboard as for being Best Supporting Actress.

The movie brought the already popular

Tchaikovsky concerto to a massively greater worldwide public that had been largely unaware of its existence and helped to invest it with the mass popularity it has enjoyed ever since.

Its nearest challenger in the classical hit parade, Rachmaninov's Piano Concerto No. 2, similarly owes its place in public affection to repeated moist-eyed accompaniment on movie soundtracks.

Ingrid Bergman played the Grieg Piano Concerto in her first Hollywood film, *Intermezzo* (1939; UK title *Escape to Happiness*).

This was a remake of an earlier Swedish movie which had brought Bergman to David Selznick's attention and his version retained the original nationality of the characters. But since no great Swedish piano concerto has yet been discovered the best alternative was to be deemed next-door neighbour Norway's Grieg.

Intermezzo carried the simple sub-title 'A Love Story' — which, indeed, it proved to be. Bergman is a piano teacher one of whose pupils is the daughter of world-famous violinist Leslie Howard.

The narcotic of music quickly engulfs them both. At one early casual encounter between them Bergman is attending the child's birthday party when she is persuaded to treat her fellow-guests to a little Grieg. Howard, even at this early stage, watches her speculatively. In turn his wife, the charming Edna Best, speculatively watches him watching Bergman. Sixth sense? She has no possible grounds for suspecting what is eventually going to evolve from the moment. But then, this is a love story.

When the inevitable happens and they become not only a romantic duo but a musical one too, Howard uses his connections to promote Bergman as a world-class concert pianist. 'You have a look in your eye of someone who has made a feast of music,' he tells her, as only the soulful hero of a musical romance knows how.

The idyll must end, of course. Bergman sends her lover back to his family with the wistful conclusion: 'I have been an intermezzo in his life.'

That such lines don't provoke a wince even now is some measure of *Intermezzo*'s affecting quality as a sob-story, slight and predictable but irridescent with Bergman's then unique freshness and sincerity.

The Tchaikovsky theme was picked up again for *Song of Russia* (1944), a movie which was of little consequence in itself but was to bring unwelcome consequences a decade later for everyone involved in it.

This was Robert Taylor's last assignment before enlisting in the US Navy. It was conceived as a propaganda boost for America's new-forged but still unlikely wartime alliance with Soviet Russia. Taylor, an avowed anti-Communist, was extremely reluctant to do it, denouncing the screenplay as 'pro-Communist sentimental hogwash'. The government's War Information Office eventually persuaded him to reconsider with an assurance that Washington was backing the movie as a friendly gesture towards the Russians.

Taylor was cast as the conductor of an American orchestra visiting the Soviet Union just

*Errol Flynn never really convinced
his action-movie fans that he
could 'compose' a ballet score for
Escape Me Never.*

prior to the 1941 Nazi invasion. He finds him-self falling in love with a beautiful young Russian concert pianist and they marry. But the advent of war, not to mention noble Commun-ist patriotism, drives a wedge between them. The girl feels duty-bound to return to her vil-lage and join the partisans.

Song of Russia launched Susan Peters, play-ing the painist, on a promising star career which was to be tragically cut short. Two years earlier she had been Oscar-nominated as Best Supporting Actress for *Random Harvest* and was viewed by her studio, MGM, as a future star asset.

But shortly after completing *Song of Russia* she was involved in a shooting accident while out hunting with her husband. Her gun dis-charged and the bullet lodged in her spine, permanently paralysing her from the waist down. She made one more film, *The Sign of the Ram*, after three years of painful rehabilitation, but in 1952 she died at the age of 31. Her doctors and friends believed she had lost the will to live.

Few movies — and certainly none as in-nocuous as *Song of Russia* — have laid up for themselves such a reputation for controversy out of all proportion to their intentions.

Robert Taylor's initial reservations about making the film came home to roost a decade later during the McCarthy witch-hunt era.

The film was cited as evidence of Communist influence at work in Hollywood during the war and Taylor testified before the House Un-American Activities Committee, recalling his objections to making it.

It must have been no less an embarrassment for him to find himself portraying a soulful artistic type in the screenplay. His performance with a baton fooled nobody, least of all profes-sional musicians, who laughed his arm-wagging to scorn.

None the less, Robert Taylor as conductor was perhaps marginally more credible than Errol Flynn as composer.

Escape Me Never (1947) was a fey, artificial affair, popular in London and New York as a play in the mid-1930s and previously filmed in Britain with some distinction. The original was bowdlerized and Hollywoodized for Flynn but musically at least it has left a distinguished legacy.

The soundtrack music was composed by Erich Wolfgang Korngold, arguably the greatest composer of film music ever to work in Holly-wood.

A child prodigy, he had been regarded as one of Europe's most precociously talented com-posers, with four successful operas to his name by the age of 30, before he fled Vienna when the Nazis annexed Austria in 1938.

113

Hollywood had already lured him over on visits, notably to score the 1936 epic *Anthony Adverse*, and he was fortuitously back there, working on the score for *The Adventures of Robin Hood*, when Hitler's stormtroopers marched into Vienna. He remained to compose some of the cinema's great scores, including *The Sea Hawk*, *The Private Lives of Elizabeth and Essex* (all, together with the earlier *Captain Blood*, highlighting a swashbuckling Errol Flynn) and *Juarez*.

He must, accordingly, have appreciated the irony of creating music for the more subdued Flynn of *Escape Me Never* to 'compose'.

To add insult to improbability, Flynn's alleged masterpiece in the story was a ballet!

Korngold wrote a short one in its entirety called *Primavera*.

Much of the plot occurs in the Alps, with Flynn looking somewhat self-conscious in Tyrolean lederhosen and cross-braces. It entangled him in a four-way love complication with his brother's heiress fiancée (Eleanor Parker) and a forlorn young unmarried mother (Ida Lupino).

Despite the heiress's blandishments, he marries the mother, giving the child a name, only to be tempted again by his prospective sister-in-law. The emoting gets under way in earnest when the baby dies, reconciling husband and wife at the very moment his ballet is having a triumphant world première.

In The Constant Nymph *Joan
Fontaine played the adoring pupil
of composer Charles Boyer.*

As a practical demonstration of Flynn's own, if meagre, musical accomplishments, one sequence allowed him to accompany a song from Ida Lupino on a squeezebox. Perhaps not surprisingly, it was the last time Korngold composed for an Errol Flynn movie.

Escape Me Never was not-quite-a-sequel to a far more substantial subject and success both as novel and play by the same author Margaret Kennedy.

In *The Constant Nymph* (1943) the central role of Lewis Dodd, another composer, was originally intended for Errol Flynn but ended up, more credibly, with Charles Boyer. It was another Korngold score and he personally performed the piano sequences heard on the soundtrack.

As in *Escape Me Never*, the composer again finds himself in the Alps, this time as tutor to the children of a Bohemian English family. One of them, the adolescent Tessa, played by Joan Fontaine, develops a mute adoration for him which will have fateful repercussions in their later lives (the character and emotions coincidentally foreshadowed Fontaine's role five years later in the more memorable *Letter from an Unknown Woman*).

Treating the girl's feelings as a passing infatuation, the composer marries a rich socialite (Alexis Smith) only to discover, too late, that his ex-pupil, now blossomed into beguiling womanhood, is the true love of his life.

'Playing Tessa in *The Constant Nymph* was the happiest motion-picture assignment of my career,' Joan Fontaine was to write 35 years later in her book *No Bed of Roses*. She adds:

'Charles Boyer remains my favourite leading man . . . a kind, gentle, helpful actor. I found him a man of intellect, taste and discernment. He was unselfish, dedicated to his work.'

There was one curious coincidence in her casting for *The Constant Nymph*. At the time of its production she was married to Brian Aherne, who had played Lewis Dodd in the British version ten years earlier. Her performance was nominated for an Academy Award.

Musical characters struck a recurring chord through the movies of both Fontaine and Boyer.

In *Break of Hearts* (1935), Boyer's second movie after settling permanently in Hollywood, he was an orchestral conductor romantically involved with Katharine Hepburn's composer (the idea of a serious woman composer was advanced, if not downright eccentric, for Hollywood in those days).

The picture, which compiled every cliché known to women's pictures, is best forgotten and duly has been. But it had one unremarked significance for the rest of Boyer's career.

He knew from past experience that his right profile photographed better than his left. In his previous film, *Private World*, his co-star Claudette Colbert had insisted on being photographed from her left side, which made it necessary for Boyer to present his right, and best, profile.

Nobody paid attention to his advice on camera angles during the *Break of Hearts* production, so he was shot from all sides and on the finished print clearly didn't look his best. The moral wasn't lost on producers. Cameramen ever after focused exclusively on his right cheek.

CHARLES BOYER
IRENE DUNNE

LOVE AFFAIR

*In the days when cinemas sold
programmes this holiday-brochure
cover hardly conveyed the bitter-
sweet quality of the shipboard
romance between violinist Charles
Boyer and Irene Dunne in* Love
Affair *(left).
The sheet-music for the remake,*
An Affair to Remember *(opposite),
caught it more evocatively.*

Two of his best roles cast him first as a violinist, in *Love Affair* (1939), then as a pianist in *When Tomorrow Comes* (1939), both opposite Irene Dunne.

Love Affair ranks as one of the classic romantic dramas. Two people meet and fall in love aboard a New York-bound liner.

Both are recovering from painful emotional experiences so, to test the strength of their feelings for each other, they part with a promise to meet again in six months' time on top of the Empire State Building.

On her way to keep the rendezvous the woman is involved in an accident and is crippled. Not wanting to be loved out of pity, she refuses to get in touch with her lover who, having waited for her in vain, bitterly writes off the affair. But fate reunites them and his understanding devotion gives her the determination to walk again.

It was unashamed sentimentality, typical of its time, transformed by director Leo McCarey's light touch into a fresh, timeless and touching masterpiece.

McCarey retrieved the screenplay and used it practically word-for-word when Cary Grant and Deborah Kerr starred in the remake, *An Affair to Remember* (1957). It is a rare example of a remake being regarded as superior to the original.

The story-line, updated, is identical to that of *Love Affair* in all but minor details. Boyer's character Michel becomes Nickie for Cary Grant. He is no longer a musician but a playboy-painter. Kerr, on the other hand, retains Dunne's original name, Terry.

The American film historian Richard Corliss considers *An Affair to Remember* to be the swan song of the genuine women's picture of its golden age, marking 'the last time a writer, a director and a pair of actors could plumb the ludicrous shallows of the weepie and emerge deliriously triumphant — and the last time Hollywood had the strength to believe in the dreams that made it great.'

When Tomorrow Comes, Charles Boyer's second musicianly role of 1939, was designed to capitalize on the success of *Love Affair* and the Dunne-Boyer chemistry.

This time he is a concert pianist, she a waitress caught up in a passionate but doomed affair shadowed by that most expedient (in those days) of script devices, a mentally unstable wife (Barbara O'Neil).

The movie inherited little of its forerunner's qualities but that didn't prevent the ingredients

being reheated eighteen years later and served up again as *Interlude* (1957).

This time it was in the care of master romantic director Douglas Sirk, but his guiding hand lacked its customary assurance.

The character of the disturbed wife survived intact; otherwise the characters and action were cosmetically remodelled in keeping with 1950s tastes. The pianist became a jet-setting conductor (Rossano Brazzi), the waitress a modish government employee working for the US Information Bureau in Munich (June Allyson).

'Fifties gloss was applied so thickly that it lacquered the romance into a fatal stiffness and the film is remembered, if at all, for its breathtaking location use of Munich, Salzburg and the Tyrol.

Joan Fontaine was at her most vulnerable and affecting as the woman with a lifelong unrequited love for pianist Louis Jourdan in Letter from an Unknown Woman.

Austria, or at any rate Vienna, could take a far greater pride in perhaps the finest of all emotion pictures structured around a musician, *Letter from an Unknown Woman* (1948).

Based on a novella by the Austrian writer Stefan Zweig, it is the tragic story of an all-consuming love-from-afar — eternal, briefly consummated but doomed by the heartrending indifference of its object.

The story unfolds in the framework of a letter to a man who, unknowingly and uncaringly, had shaped the sad destiny of its writer.

Stefan Brand is a concert pianist whose dashing looks and brilliant artistry captivate the teenage daughter of a widow living in a neighbouring apartment.

As the film opens he is preparing to respond to a duelling challenge. The delivery of the

119

letter delays him and as he reads it the writer's voice unfolds a tragic story.

For the gauche, sensitive Lisa a schoolgirl crush intensifies into a lifelong passion. 'Though you didn't know it, you were giving me some of the happiest hours of my life,' she writes.

Grown into a beautiful woman, she rejects a suitable arranged marriage, forsakes her mother and dedicates her life to adoration of a celebrity whose only words to her have been to pass the time of day.

Finally he becomes aware of her and, although she knows she is only the latest novelty in a succession of casual mistresses, she submits to him ecstatically.

After a few hours of rapture he leaves the country for a concert engagement, promising to return to her in two weeks. It is many years before she sees him again.

She has borne his son and married a wealthy older man who accepts her past. At the opera one night the lovers' paths cross once more.

'The course of our lives can be changed by such little things,' she writes. 'I know now that nothing happens by chance. Every moment is measured, every step is counted.'

The pianist is by now burned out artistically and morally, but Lisa sees only the man she wants to see until, having accepted his invitation back to his apartment, she realizes he doesn't remember her. She is just another pretty face from his past.

While he is absent from the room she quietly slips out of his life. Returning home, she finds her son stricken with a sudden illness — fate has cruelly twisted its knife in her wounds even while was she re-opening them with her illicit assignation. The boy has typhus and dies. She too has unknowingly caught the virus.

As Stefan, remorse stealing over him for the first time in his life, turns to the final page of the letter the handwriting trails away in mid-sentence. She too is dead. It is her husband who now waits for Stefan to meet his challenge.

The great German director Max Ophuls fashioned this slender tragedy into a delicate, hushed miniature, creating a mood of rarefied romanticism and drawing beautiful performances from his two stars.

Joan Fontaine, cast again in a part as a timorous adolescent (she had turned 30 at the time) was never more touchingly vulnerable, her performance alive to every gossamer nuance of youthful unrequited love. Louis Jourdan gauged perfectly the shallow charm and self-interest of Stefan.

It was Jourdan's second Hollywood film. With his Gallic good looks, soulful eyes and seductive but reassuring voice, he was being groomed as the natural successor to an ageing Charles Boyer. That his career subsequently failed to follow a similar course owed more to Hollywood's misjudgement of the roles and movies allocated to him than to any deficiency in his capacity to be a Boyer-clone. Only once after *Letter from an Unknown Woman* did the hoped-for qualities gell perfectly — in *Gigi*.

As it is, the Ophuls film, so exquisitely capturing the romantic mystique of Hapsburg Vienna, stands as a landmark in the career of both stars — 'probably the toniest [high-tone] women's picture ever made' in the judgement of Pauline Kael.

Three years later Joan Fontaine was herself a concert pianist in *September Affair* (1950), an affair remembered only for a quirky musical factor. Its theme tune was 'September Song', salvaged from the 1938 Broadway musical *Knickerbocker Holiday* in which it had been sung by actor Walter Huston. No singer, he, but his old recording of it reverberated through the soundtrack, becoming a much-loved hit because of, rather than in spite of, his querulous vocal display.

'Shooting the film was pleasant,' Miss Fontaine recalled in her book, a memory no doubt coloured by her stated relief at escaping to Europe on location from a complicated romantic situation of her own.

Her three-year marriage to RKO studio head William Dozier was heading for the divorce court and she had resumed her on-off involvement with Howard Hughes. ('Again Howard proposed. Again I sensed that marriage to this eccentric recluse, now almost totally deaf, would be plunging into an unknown abyss. I declined.')

The movie, according to its star, was 'a delightful escapist romance'. She played a celebrated pianist, Joseph Cotten a successful architect. They are fellow passengers on a plane who, sightseeing in Naples during a stopover,

manage to miss their flight and hence the subsequent crash which kills everyone on board.

When a casualty list is published with their names on it they realize they are free of all previous responsibilities and can start a new life together under assumed identities.

Rachmaninov surged and swelled. Happiness on such fraudulent terms could not, however, be countenanced under the Hollywood Code. Conscience (his) and career (hers) finally prise them apart and back to their senses, but not before the travelogue potential

An old, half-forgotten song took on a new lease of popularity when it was resurrected as the theme music for September Affair.

of Florence, Venice, Naples and Capri has been fully exploited.

The director, William Dieterle, had dabbled successfully in this kind of emotional business with two earlier Joseph Cotten vehicles, *Love Letters* and *I'll Be Seeing You*. This, his last exercise in the style, did not complete a hat-trick of successes, however. It served its glossy heartache purpose adequately enough but was altogether too slick for its own good. Walter Huston's arthritic singing ironically outlived the film.

Italy again provided a musical hothouse atmosphere for *Rhapsody* (1954); Rachmaninov and Tchaikovsky again contributed the music.

Few romances have been more overwrought — indeed, this was positively operatic in its passion levels, even if the soundtrack idiom is strictly instrumental.

The movie is an anthem to Elizabeth Taylor's 22-year-old beauty; never, until then, had it been more sumptuously ogled by colour cameras.

Unfortunately it required little else of her except showy displays of petulance as a spoiled little rich girl set down distractingly among students at a music conservatory.

Two of the most attractive are caught in her grasping toils to their artistic cost, violinist Vittorio Gassman and pianist John Ericson. Constantly craving attention from one or the other, Taylor plays havoc with their studies and selfishly keeps them from practising.

Gassman at least has the strength of character and will to make her play second fiddle to his Stradivarius and so ensures he becomes a Great Artist in spite of their Great Love.

It is pianist Ericson who succumbs to her blandishments and, ultimately, the bottle.

One of the more enduring memories of the movie is the spectacle of Gassman, all frowns and artistic integrity, practising ferociously while Taylor tickles his ears and twiddles her fingers in his abundant hair.

Newsweek reported that she 'swoons beautifully to the airs of Peter Illyitch Tchaikovsky and Sergei Rachmaninov . . . in a women's picture de luxe.'

The *New York Herald Tribune*, on the other hand, grouchily concluded that

> the point of the whole story is to show off Elizabeth Taylor wearing attractive gowns, sobbing in loneliness or radiant at a concert . . . it looks as though Miss Taylor's charms had struck everyone senseless, leaving nothing but this charm for the movie to go on.

The apotheosis of the musical women's picture has to be *Deception* (1946), which reunited the quartet who had ensured such success for *Now, Voyager* four years earlier: Irving Rapper directing; Bette Davis as Christine Radcliffe, a pianist; Paul Henreid as Karel Novak, a cellist; Claude Rains as Alexander Hollenius, *the* great composer!

Bette Davis on the set of Deception with the distinguished composer Erich Wolfgang Korngold (right). The concerto that Korngold composed for Davis's cellist husband Paul Henreid to perform in Deception sets the scene for the emotional turmoil that follows (below).

123

The tempo was overwrought, the emotions *fortissimo*. The movie won the cinema equivalent of a standing ovation from the public if not the critics.

We first encounter Davis, youthfully rapt (she was actually 39) and moist-eyed in the back row of a concert hall, listening to Novak perform the final bars of a Haydn concerto.

Later, waiting anonymously until well-wishers have left his dressing-room, she stands in the doorway like a symbol of fate, her face distorted with rampant emotions, and delivers her first line on an anguished wail: 'I thought you were *dead*.'

It seems they had been passionately in love and on the point of marriage as music students in Vienna years before, but the war had torn them apart and Novak had been sent to a concentration camp.

Back home in New York, meanwhile, she has adopted the professional name by which she is now moderately well known (neatly explaining Novak's failure to find her in the phone book).

She has also become the mistress of Hollenius, who, being a Great Composer, is addressed or referred to by his surname only throughout.

The original French play on which *Deception* was based was called *Jealousy*, which gives a more concise interpretation of what it is about.

Novak, trying to equate the extravagance of her apartment, furs, jewels and tastes with her modest earning capacity, rightly suspects she is a kept woman. To divert him from the truth, Christine proposes they go ahead immediately with the long-delayed wedding. Hollenius, learning of it belatedly, storms the reception to wither them both, and presumably their nuptial night, with his jealous scorn.

It so happens that he has just completed a cello concerto and, being equally a maestro of Machiavellian guile, offers Novak the honour of giving its première performance, an opportunity which will make his name.

Christine, however, guesses what he is up to. Hollenius, personally conducting the performances, plans to humiliate his rival in public. When appeals to his better nature fail to dissuade him, she shoots him dead on the grand staircase of his improbably grandiose mansion.

As one critic of the times remarked: 'It's like grand opera only the people are thinner . . . I wouldn't have missed it for the world,' while for Pauline Kael it is 'blissfully foolish . . . a camp classic'.

In a generally subdued performance of controlled hysteria Bette Davis's finest moments follow her decision to take matters and a revolver into her own hands for the finale. She blends ruthless iciness and vulnerability in a mesmeric display of resolution, guilt and redeeming self-sacrifice.

It's the only part of the film when any of its three characters elicit a gust of audience sympathy. They are otherwise thoroughly shallow, self-centred and disagreeable specimens.

But at least, in Hollenius, Claude Rains created one of his most vivid characterizations. Bette Davis is on record as saying: 'The picture wasn't terribly good but he was brilliant.'

There was brilliance, too, in the music. Erich

Wolfgang Korngold composed a piecemeal cello concerto, fragments of which recur throughout the soundtrack. Later he expanded it into a complete work which periodically gets aired in concert halls. In the film's opening sequence he can be glimpsed conducting the Haydn concerto himself.

The scenes of Paul Henreid's cello-playing were a masterstroke of cinematographic trickery. His hands were tied behind his back. A specially designed coat concealed not one but two professional cellists crouched behind him. The left arm of one through the appropriate sleeve took care of the bowing, the right arm of the other performed the fingering. With foreknowledge it's possible to fancy that the cut of Henreid's coat is on the baggy side but visually the trick comes off perfectly in Irving Rapper's carefully plotted camera angles.

Herself no mean pianist, Bette Davis was only once required to demonstrate at the keyboard. She begins to play Beethoven's 'Appassionata' Sonata — what else in these circumstances? — during the fateful wedding reception.

She practised it for three hours a day and wanted to record it herself for the soundtrack. Director Rapper vetoed this suggestion on the grounds that 'no one will believe you actually performed the number anyway'. The distinguished concert pianist Shura Cherkassky stood in for her. Davis's on-camera fingerwork is impeccable, nonetheless.

Not to be outdone by her arch rival, Joan Crawford that same year set her formidable passions to music for *Humoresque* (1946).

Her performance as a selfish, wealthy but loveless wife with nymphomaniacal and alcoholic tendencies who orchestrates the career of a brilliant young violinist is often cited as quintessential Crawford, the finest she delivered. Certainly she was at the height of her powers, psyched up on the new-found confidence and upturn in career which *Mildred Pierce* and an Oscar had just brought her. The role of Helen Wright is the classic Crawford image that has passed into movie mythology.

The musician Paul Borey, played with hardly less intensity by John Garfield, is also classic — the artist for whom art transcends all other considerations.

He is the latest plaything of a woman whose sexual appetite has chewed up a string of adulterous lovers. With this one she falls genuinely in love, probably because she senses he is a man who refuses to be dominated, owned or trifled with.

As the tempestuous affair develops Helen uses her social connections to advance his career but, though he loves her, Paul can't handle her demanding nature. They quarrel and split. When they meet again Helen, chastened, realizes the destructive power of her possessiveness.

She is due to attend one of his concerts. Instead she stays home and listens to it on the radio. Only Hollywood could contrive to have him perform the Liebestod ('love-death'), from Wagner's *Tristan and Isolde*, a work never intended for violin soloist nor ever played in such a way except on this occasion.

As the great hymn of ecstasy Isolde sings over

658-52

the body of Tristan before they are reunited in death fades away, Helen walks out of the house and into the nearby ocean, much as Norman Maine does in *A Star is Born*.

'Hokey weeper', pronounced Pauline Keal, though she conceded it had some effective elements ... 'some of the dialogue is sharp-witted'.

No matter! Audiences lapped up its wholly improbable plot (from a story by that *grande dame* of tear-jerking, Fannie Hurst) and glamorous production values.

John Garfield was unanimously praised for his expert fiddling. It was not generally realized that the *Deception* deception was again pressed into service for his actual playing, two violinists behind his back, each with an arm through his coat sleeves. The illusion was completed by the great violinist Isaac Stern on the sound-track.

Roy Newquist, in his book *Conversations with Joan Crawford*, quotes her as saying: 'John Garfield ... did a fine job. He was so much the young, struggling musician I think the audience felt he really played the violin himself.'

Of her own performance she wasn't so sure. 'Most of the time I thought I was doing well but when I finally saw it ... I cringed.

'I overacted and over-reacted in so many scenes. I don't know. I should have done better.'

Few, then or since, have agreed with her. *Humoresque* is one of her most memorable performances.

The following year, 1947, abruptly sounded the last chord for the 'forties cycle of 'music equals class' titles. Neatly, and not without an unintended irony, the fad took its final bow with one of its best examples, *Letter from an Unknown Woman*, and probably the most pretentiously absurd of any it spawned.

Night Song (1947) runs the gamut of clichés. Dana Andrews is both brilliant pianist and composer. He is also blind, the result of an accident, and bitter because the affliction forces him to abandon the great concerto he has long been working on.

Tiptoeing in Joan Crawford's *Humoresque* footsteps, Merle Oberon is a millionairess with a mission to save him from himself and for Art. Knowing he won't accept her charity, she devises an unnecessarily complicated plan of action to win his trust and love. She pretends not only to be blind herself but poor as well.

On the quiet she puts up the money for a major competition and badgers him to enter. Naturally, she makes sure he wins and he uses the prize money for an operation to restore his sight.

One look at Oberon, the haute-coutured socialite, and he is hooked into a passionate affair. Belatedly he remembers the poor little blind girl who had meant so much to him and remorse consumes him. This presents Oberon with a delicate personality problem which she overcomes — as if anyone wouldn't guess — on the evening his now completed concerto has its triumphant première. He realizes that the two women in his life are, in fact, one and the same — the well-heeled manifestation, happily.

The inevitable rehearsal chore of mastering the keyboard fingerwork fell particularly hard

Joan Crawford counted the cost of investing more than money in her violinist protégé John Garfield in Humoresque.

on Dana Andrews. He was required to achieve authenticity while affecting not to be able to see what he was doing.

The saddest thing about *Night Song* was that its director was the veteran John Cromwell, nearing the close of an illustrious career dotted with such classics as the Leslie Howard–Bette Davis *Of Human Bondage*, the Ronald Colman version of *The Prisoner of Zenda, Since You Went Away* and *Anna and the King of Siam*.

The best thing about it was its soundtrack. The great Artur Rubinstein was hired to perform the concerto on-camera with the New York Philharmonic Orchestra at Carnegie Hall as well as dubbing all the hero's other pianistic feats elsewhere in the screenplay.

The concerto itself was specially composed by Leith Stevens. The *New York Times* mischievously sent its music critic along to the movie to review the opus. He found it 'as slick as ice and just about as stable'!

The name of Victor Schertzinger contributes a unique footnote to this recital as it does to the history of movies. An unsung veteran, he was the only known example of a Hollywood composer-director.

Pennsylvania-born, he studied music in Brussels and acquired a modest reputation around European capitals as a concert violinist before returning to the United States to conduct musical comedies. He made his Hollywood début in 1916 and later branched out into directing.

His greatest success was *One Night of Love*, the 1934 musical which made an international star of opera singer Grace Moore and launched the vogue for opera/film stars like Lily Pons, Gladys Swarthout and the everlastingly popular duets between Jeanette MacDonald and Nelson Eddy.

This breakthrough movie won Schertzinger a unique Oscar double with nominations for Best Director and Best Picture and an award for the title song.

He went on to direct the first two of the Hope-Crosby-Lamour *Road* films — *The Road to Singapore* and *The Road to Zanzibar*; and he both directed and wrote the songs for the hit musical *The Fleet's In*, which included two of Betty Hutton's classic numbers, 'Build a Better

Merle Oberon was another rich woman who paid the price for falling in love with a musician in Night Song.

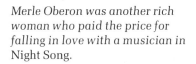

One-man-band Victor Schertzinger both directed and composed Beloved (below).

Mousetrap' and 'Arthur Murray Taught Me Dancing in a Hurry'. It was his last film, released posthumously.

But the film dearest to his musical heart was probably a forgotten weepie, *Beloved* (1934).

A tear-stained four-generation family saga, it chronicled the life and loves of composer Carl Haussmann, who flees Vienna at the height of the 1848 revolution and fetches up in South Carolina.

After serving in the Civil War, he marries a long-suffering, though understanding, Gloria Stuart and scratches a living in New York teaching the violin (one of his pupils was the 14-year-old Mickey Rooney, only months away from stardom as Puck in *A Midsummer Night's Dream*).

Their son turns out to be something of a black sheep and is killed in the Spanish-American War, but his young grandson inherits the bloodline's musical spark and, under Grandpa's tutelage, shows the makings of genius.

Through all this angst Carl has been working on his Great Symphony, completing it in the nick of time so that he can die happy after hearing it received in rapture at its première.

Playing Carl provided a no doubt welcome respite from gentlemanly cads and charming rotters for John Boles, whose good looks and sonorous voice had made him one of the most in-demand and popular romantic leads of that time. Alas, he was also one of the most wooden actors of that time and the idea of his mustering sufficient passion to devote lifelong to composing a symphony was not least among the film's implausibilities.

6

Silent Suffering

WHEN GARBO WAS SEEN DYING at the end of *Camille* there were some in its audiences who claimed they had glimpsed the soul leave her body. That their emotions had been so totally engaged as to convince them they had seen the impossible is a tribute to the film's power of suggestiveness and Garbo's technique.

The illusion, for those who imagined it, was created by a simple but daring device on Garbo's part. Lying, weakly ecstatic, in her lover's arms with her eyes closed, she just fluttered them open at the moment of death. Millions headed homeward crying happily.

No human condition elicits sympathy or touches the heart more sincerely than illness quietly and nobly endured.

Camille, doomed from the start by the consumption which will snuff out the gaiety and beauty she represents as a courtesan and her last chance of true love and decent values, for which she has renounced her old life, survives as the goddess symbol of long-suffering heroines.

In movies they have always born their afflictions with fortitude and, if the script required them to die, they died selflessly and beautifully.

Camille appropriately died most beautifully of all, her wan, wasted (but not too wasted) face irradiated by the lighting cameraman.

Since it would have traduced all the hallowed articles of movie-making to disfigure a heroine (or hero, for that matter), fatal illness needed to be of an internal, non-visible nature. Consumption, tuberculosis, heart disease,

blindness and deafness were therefore the preferred disabilities. A slight ravaging of the face not only touches the emotions but enhances a received impression of suffering by infusing it with a haunting quality.

Besides, hollowed cheeks photograph so well.

There's a sound exploitative case for illness in romance too, of course. Apart from parading moral courage and shining spirituality in the victim, it brings out correspondingly fine instincts in the victim's partner.

Facing death nobly: Bette Davis with George Brent in Dark Victory *(opposite) and Greta Garbo with Robert Taylor, in* Camille *(right).*

131

SILENT SUFFERING

A husband or lover, unless he is a louse (and therefore not a hero-figure), becomes supportive, more devoted than ever and often emotionally dependent without compromising his masculinity. There is no surer way to a woman's heart.

It helps, too, if the illness has been diagnosed *before* the partners fall in love. As a dramatic means for heightening sensibilities there is nothing to match the knowledge that the time in which to enjoy happiness is fleeting.

One of the earliest talkies to make use of it, *One Way Passage* (1932), screwed the emotional effect even tighter by confining the love affair to an ocean liner for the all-too-limited duration of a voyage from Hong Kong to San Francisco.

On the passenger list are Kay Francis, suffering from incurable heart disease although never looking less than ravishingly elegant, and William Powell, a convicted murderer returning home in custody to face execution.

Neither knows the other's problem until the ship calls at Honolulu and Francis suffers a heart attack while they are ashore.

The prisoner forfeits his only chance to escape so that he can carry her back aboard. Told that a sudden shock could be fatal for her, he keeps his own secret from her with the connivance of his detective escort.

She discovers the truth about him when they dock at San Francisco but, in the tradition of such heroines, conceals her heartbreak and promises to meet him at an appointed place on New Year's Eve. It's a date neither can keep.

The movie's closing shot sealed its high-quality weepiness with symbolic perfection. Two champagne glasses on a bar touch and shatter.

One Way Passage is one of the most fondly remembered romances of the 'thirties, sensitively scripted and directed and with poised performances from Kay Francis and William Powell. It won an Academy Award for Best Original Story.

There were no Oscars, however, for the remake of eight years later, *Till We Meet Again* (1940), though Merle Oberon gave a delicately touching performance opposite George Brent. She unknowingly suffered herself from a heart condition which would cause her death in 1980 at the age of 69.

She was assigned to the role after it had been turned down by Bette Davis, who was reluctant to suffer another incurable illness so soon after *Dark Victory* (1939).

The moment when Bette Davis realizes death is near, in Dark Victory *with Geraldine Fitzgerald.*

In that classic tear-jerker Davis garnered her third Oscar nomination in the year Vivien Leigh won the award for *Gone with the Wind*. The film itself was nominated for Best Picture.

By today's standards her performance as wealthy, wilful Judith Traherne seems brittle. Even in its day the movie was guardedly reviewed as 'emotional flimflam' expertly assembled and served. But time has been kind to it and while there is no avoiding its frontal assault on the tear-ducts (and who would want to?) it carries the hallmark of high-grade Hollywood.

Judith is a personable, popular member of Long Island's social set, loving life and any man who cares to court her and troubled only by recurring headaches.

Concerned friends engineer a meeting with an eminent specialist, Dr Frederick Steele (George Brent), who surreptitiously carries out some simple test, arousing her interest in him but not suspicions of his ulterior motive.

He diagnoses a brain tumour and urges immediate surgery, though aware that it will only give her brief remission. By now she has fallen in love with him but, accidentally learning she has only a year to live, angrily rejects his proposal of marriage and embarks on a riotous 'today I must live for tomorrow I die' round of high-living.

She is made to see the error of her ways by, of all unlikely characters, Humphrey Bogart as a stable groom who has worshipped her from afar. He convinces her that she should seize what happiness time and the fates have allotted her, so she marries her doctor and they retire to the simple life in his Connecticut farm for the few months left to her.

Thus the scene is set for one of the most moving death scenes in movies.

Steele is away for the weekend at a medical conference, leaving Judith in the care of her staunch secretary/friend (Geraldine Fitzgerald). She is contentedly planting hyacinths in the garden when she remarks that the sky is clouding over. Yet she can still feel the sun on her face. She realizes that with the approach of blindness death is near.

Bravely she comforts the stricken friend and climbs the stairs to her room to face the end alone but grateful for the brief months of happiness she has known.

It is a rare elegiac interlude in Bette Davis's gallery of impetuous heroines and she has never played a finer scene.

'Eloquence, tenderness and heart-breaking

A poignant study (opposite) of Susan Hayward, prepared for death from a brain tumour in Stolen Hours, a remake of Dark Victory. *She would courageously face her own death from the same cause twelve years later.*

sincerity' was how the *New York Times* lauded her performance, and of the film it commented: 'It is impossible to be cynical about it. The mood is too poignant, the performances too honest, the craftsmanship too perfect.'

It was the first film to give a young actor a foot-hold in what he would much later call 'upper-crust picture-making'. Ronald Reagan played one of Judith's fast-set suitors.

His memories of it, recorded in his autobiography, *My Early Life*, 26 years later, are tinged with regret that he muffed his one big scene.

He shared it with George Brent, and director Edmund Goulding reprimanded the future President of the United States: 'Do you think you are playing the leading man? George has that part, you know.' Reagan claims he bowed to Goulding's authority and played it as directed. 'I ended up not delivering the line the way my instinct told me it should be delivered. It was bad.'

Dark Victory was remade in England as *Stolen Hours* (1963), a slick, conveyor-belt model of considerable gloss but not much heart until that final fail-safe scene.

Susan Hayward, at 47, could hardly be expected to recapture the devil-may-care zest Bette Davis, at 30, had brought to the role, sparking it instead with her trademark drive of fiery 'damn the lot of you' truculence.

But those last hours, this time in a cottage overlooking the Cornish cliffs, carried a poignancy every bit as effective as the original had and Hayward's quiet dignity was the equal of Davis's.

Unknown then to her or anyone watching her, the character was a harrowing presentiment of the suffering and courage with which she would later meet her own death.

Susan Hayward developed multiple brain tumours. Given six months to live in 1973, she fought back with all the guts she had poured into her roles and endured two more years of punishing pain.

Her last public appearance, against all medical advice, at the 1974 Academy Award ceremony to present the Best Actress Award to Glenda Jackson, was a triumph of will-power. Walking with difficulty on the arm of Charlton Heston, she presented an image of star glamour which had taken make-up artist Frank Westmore six painstaking hours to create.

In a sense she was that night a vindication of that article of Hollywood faith which held that the eye should not be offended by suffering or disfigurement.

Westmore, recalling the day, wrote afterwards:

I was distressed at what I saw. Susan had been undergoing radioactive cobalt treatment for a malignant brain tumour and the damaging rays had destroyed her beautiful red hair, her eyebrows, even her eyelashes. The basic pert and beautiful face was still there but I had to reconstruct her as she had been thirty years before.

I was never more proud of my craftsmanship than when I saw Susan walk out on that stage . . . She looked not much different from the Susan Hayward of 1945 and that's how the world will remember her.

SILENT SUFFERING

Ronald Reagan's own hour of stoic screen suffering would come after the war when he had achieved his own star billing. In *Night unto Night* (1949), a film curiously overlooked by the President's satirists, he is a scientist terminally stricken with epilepsy. He enters into a hesitant relationship with a widow (Viveca Lindfors), whose mental illness is the result of rather improbably finding the body of her naval officer husband washed up on the beach near their home after he has been killed in action.

The film's fledgling director was Don Siegel who, 20 years later, was to find himself more at home and a box-office tyro directing Clint Eastwood's *Dirty Harry* films.

One callous critic dismissed *Night unto Night* as a 'boring, tiresome melodrama about the romance of two characters who'd be better off dead'.

The most enduring of all the titles which have wrung tears and heartache out of a medical condition is *Magnificent Obsession* (1935),

Robert Taylor rocketed to stardom as the young doctor whose surgical skills and undying love save the life of the woman whose husband he has accidentally killed, in Magnificent Obsession.

filmed twice and each time coincidentally promoting a small-part actor into a new heart-throb male star.

The first version brought fame to a 24-year-old Robert Taylor who, on the strength of this first starring role, was voted the screen's top male personality the following year.

The screenplay, based on Lloyd C. Douglas's massive best-seller, formulates all the trite improbabilities so scorned in women's pictures. It is the legerdemain of director John M. Stahl, a wily veteran of the species, which makes them not only plausible but deeply affecting.

Bobby Merrick is a young tearaway involved in an accident which costs the life of a much-respected doctor. Chastened, he tries to express his apologies to the widow, Helen (Irene Dunne), but when she tries to flee from his unwanted attentions she is run down by a car and loses her sight.

The multiple tragedy determines Bobby to atone by completing his own medical studies so that he can become a surgeon and cure her blindness. In the meantime he wins her trust without her guessing who he is. Love follows, but when she realizes his true identity she rejects him, secretly afraid of her own feelings, and walks out of his life.

Years pass in which Bobby has fulfilled his vow and become a successful surgeon, haunted by memories of Helen. Then, miraculously, he finds her again in a hospital, her condition

Ronald Reagan stoically suffered from epilepsy, sharing afflictions with a mentally ill Viveca Lindfors in Night Unto Night (opposite).

worse than ever. Only a delicate operation can save her. Only one surgeon is prepared to take the risk!

The outcome blurred the vision of audiences worldwise. Helen is coming out of anaesthetic. Her eyes flutter open. She blinks. A milky light fills the screen. A formless image slowly clarifies into the features of Bobby bending over her, his eyes alight with love . . .

Magnificent Obsession was one of the ten top money-making films of 1935. More surprisingly still, it repeated the trick with the more cynical audiences of 1954 when the remake ranked No. 7 among the box-office hits.

This second time around it even netted an Oscar nomination for Jane Wyman. Star excitement, however, focused on Rock Hudson. Repeating the process which had made Robert Taylor an overnight sensation, he won the lead role after serving his time in bit parts and B-westerns or swashbuckler leads. The female public's reaction was as instantaneous as it had been to Taylor. Two years later he would be

137

nominated for a Best Actor Oscar for *Giant*; another two years and *Look Magazine* would name him Star of the Year.

Magnificent Obsession launched producer Ross Hunter's glossy revival of tried-and-tested 'thirties weepies, including *Imitation of Life, Back Street* and *Madame X*. His formula was simple but shrewd — leave the tear-jerking mechanism intact but dress and trim it to look expensive and sophisticated for a more discerning generation of filmgoers.

He used the original screenplay for his *Magnificent Obsession* remake, merely updating it, drenching it with vibrant colour and making minor concessions to modern idiom — the Bobby of 1935, for example, became the more hunky Bob for 1954.

Consideration for the Academy Award had by this time become something of a knee-jerk reaction to any Jane Wyman performance. *Magnificent Obsession* brought her fourth nomination, six years after she had won the Best Actress Oscar for *Johnny Belinda* (1948).

Wyman was an exception to the rule that afflicted heroines should not be permitted to sacrifice their looks. She had already deglamourized herself convincingly for *The Yearling* — earning one of her Oscar nominations — and went even further in *Johnny Belinda* by assuming a scissored, unkempt hairstyle, homespun clothing, a totally self-effacing presence and using no make-up.

The impact of her performance was all the more striking because, playing a deaf-mute, she was left with no means of self-expression other than her eyes and mouth.

Belinda, deaf and dumb since birth, has been brought up by her widowed father and his sister on a rugged Nova Scotia farm where the living is meagre and she is treated little better than one of the animals.

A new doctor (Lew Ayres) who takes a sympathetic interest in her case teaches her sign language and lip-reading, opening up a world of new experience to her.

Growing self-awareness brings about an improvement in appearance and manner and the locals begin to treat her as a human being rather than as 'the dummy', the soubriquet by which she has always been known.

One night she is raped by the village braggart (Stephen McNally) and when she gives birth to a son, Johnny, the doctor is suspected of being the father.

The rapist meanwhile has married the village belle (and the doctor's receptionist) and decides he wants custody of 'his' child. As he attempts to take it by force Belinda seizes her father's shotgun and shoots him dead.

At the subsequent trial the truth emerges and Belinda, doctor and Johnny are left free to start a new life together.

More drama than weepie, *Johnny Belinda* nevertheless goes straight to the heart, most searchingly in the profoundly moving scene in

Magnificent Obsession *also made a new heart-throb star of Rock Hudson when he was teamed in the remake with Jane Wyman (opposite, above).*

Jane Wyman won everyone's heart and an Oscar for her sensitive performance as a tragic deaf-mute in Johnny Belinda *(opposite, below).*

A 1944 studio publicity still of Loretta Young, who played the deaf heroine of that year's film And Now Tomorrow.

which Belinda 'says' the Lord's Prayer in sign language over the body of her father, killed in a brawl by the rapist.

Perhaps because of its connotations of stupidity, deafness has never been a popular means of soliciting sympathy in movies. But one star, Loretta Young, courageously subjected herself to it twice, first in the 1939 biopic *The Story of Alexander Graham Bell.*

More emotionally, *And Now Tomorrow* (1944) used the disability as a trip-wire for that time-honoured plot device of women's pictures, the patient who falls in love with her doctor. And as if one cliché were not enough, another was grafted on. The two characters come from opposite sides of the tracks in a small New England community.

An attack of meningitis on the night of her engagement party robs Emily Blair, daughter of the town's leading family, of her hearing.

The engagement is put on ice while she makes a slow recovery, but the illness leaves her totally deaf. Her fiancé Jeff (Barry Sullivan)

is not so slow, meanwhile, in appreciating the charms of her kid sister Janice, who has returned home for the celebrations; hers is a character tailored to the deceitful nature in which Susan Hayward specialized at that formative stage of her career.

It so happens that Dr Merek Vance (Alan Ladd) has recently developed an as-yet-untried serum for just this kind of hearing condition. Moreover he happens to have grown up in the same small town on the other side of the tracks, regarding the sister with class-conscious awe and not a little resentment.

He reluctantly agrees to treat Emily but, inevitably, they don't take to each other until one night when he is called to an emergency case. She chances to be with him and acquits herself nobly in administering an anaesthetic.

Emily finally persuades Dr Vance to try the serum on her. So far it has only worked on deaf rabbits! For days she wavers between life and deaf. But it works. Her hearing is restored.

Janice, who knows this, engineers a confrontation with Jeff, who doesn't, outside Emily's bedroom door and tells him, in a loud voice, that they must renounce their love for each other for Emily's sake. This mean little ruse has the desired effect. Emily realizes it is the doctor she truly loves, which goes to show that deceit brings its own rewards.

'A very stupid little movie', thought the *New York Times*. But a public avid to see Alan Ladd in his first sympathetic role following his leap to stardom in *This Gun for Fire* and *The Glass Key* thought otherwise and made it one of the year's top successes.

The movie has one claim to historical curiosity. Its slightly mawkish screenplay was co-authored by that master of hard-boiled dialogue Raymond Chandler, the only romantic script he ever worked on.

Hollywood's insistence on displaying its stars to their best unblemished advantage regardless of any indisposition the characters they portrayed may be suffering marred Barbara Stanwyck's detour into latter-day Camille territory in *The Other Love* (1947).

Its director Andre de Toth has recalled:

The picture was shot in late 1946/early 1947. At that time the motion picture industry was still shackled to Hollywood. We who were seeking reality not only in portraying characters but also in presenting true geographical locations had great difficulties and many obstacles to overcome.

Even a star as thoroughgoing and influential as Barbara Stanwyck couldn't overcome the obstacle of over-glamourization.

The Other Love packed in as many of the regulation women's-picture clichés as a slender storyline could support.

A famed concert pianist stricken with tuberculosis . . . conflict with her doctor transfigured into love . . . a death-defying last fling with a tearaway racing driver . . . reconciliation with doctor and destiny.

It fulfilled all the conventions of the genre: vicariously romantic, glamorous settings and wardrobe, smatterings of culture and medical mystique, a quasi-classical soundtrack score. But convincing, never.

The performances at least were wholehearted as was to be expected from Stanwyck as the pianist Karen Duncan and David Niven as the doctor. Their love/hate-nest was an exclusive sanitorium high in the Swiss Alps with an excursion to Monte Carlo for Karen's AWOL affair with racing driver Richard Conte.

Miss Stanwyck, Camille-like, coughed occasionally; otherwise she seemed, to all appearances, as robust as Phyllis Dietrichson or Martha Ivers.

In the end, having learned the humility of love, she marries her doctor who, when she finally expires, sends her, serene and fulfilled, on her way by playing Chopin on the grand piano in her hospital suite.

The film was based on a short story by Erich Maria Remarque, author of *All Quiet on the Western Front*. He wrung impressive mileage out of it. The same theme, amplified, reappeared fourteen years later as his novel *Heaven Has No Favourites*, which in its turn inspired the 1977 movie *Bobby Deerfield*.

SILENT SUFFERING

Hollywood studios fought shy of releasing publicity stills of their stars looking plain or disfigured but an exception was made for Robert Young and Dorothy McGuire in The Enchanted Cottage.

The romantic interest in this variation centred on the incurable heroine, now an anything-goes swinger in tune with the 'sixties, and a racing driver, played by Marthe Keller and Al Pacino. The background remained picturesquely Central European.

Taboos had long been breached when *Bobby Deerfield* — in no sense a remake of *The Other Love* — appeared. Yet there are certain cinematic conventions, particularly in the women's picture, which die hard. The 1970s heroine may be liberated to the degree, unthinkable in her 1940s predecessor, of inviting her new-found lover into her bed. But they were both still sisters under the skin. They shared an 'incurable disease' which left their looks unscathed and they died with ethereal beauty.

There was, however, one isolated case in the 'forties of a movie allowing not only its heroine but also its hero to be seen facially disfigured, albeit as a plot device with assurance their good looks would be restored.

The Enchanted Cottage (1945), based on a play by Sir Arthur Wing Pinero, visualized the old adage that 'beauty is in the eye of the beholder'.

Robert Young is a wartime flier whose face has been scarred, Dorothy McGuire a repressed young woman whose life has been blighted by her ugly duckling looks. They are introduced by a composer (Herbert Marshall) — there was no escaping classy art in the 'forties — who appoints himself their 'guardian angel'.

Feeling themselves to be outcast, they marry and set up home in the cottage of the title. Its magical property lies in transforming the inner

beauty of their souls and suffering into a visible
external beauty, at which point the stars have
their familiar facial features restored.

Once, when an unthinking action by the
flier's mother reveals them to each other as
outsiders see them, their sanctuary from reality
is threatened. But the power of love and mutual
dependence renews their illusion.

Sentimental, but it was directed with tenderness by that skilled romantic John Cromwell
and acted sincerely by Young and McGuire.

Sentimentality was strained to its zenith (or
nadir, depending on the degree of audience
cynicism) the following year in the uncom-
promisingly titled *Sentimental Journey* (1946.

Maureen O'Hara dies of heart disease half-
way through the running time, to return a few
reels later and for the rest of the footage as a
ghost. Each of her manifestations thereafter is
heralded by tinkling bells!

Julie is a famous actress married to Broadway
producer Bill (John Payne), who doesn't know
about her illness. She longs for a child but it
would be fatal for her to get pregnant. In any

144

case Bill is pretty childish himself in the way he depends on her for everything.

Realizing he could be left alone and helpless at any moment, she persuades him into adopting an orphaned moppet. 'I thought she might help him to grow up; look after him, too,' she explains to a friend.

The dialogue, as it wafts into rarefied layers of philosophizing, is one of the film's chief, if unintentional, entertainments.

Julie tells the child: 'We all live more or less by our dreams. I think people like you and me would die if we couldn't dream.'

Maureen O'Hara succumbs to her fatal heart condition in the arms of husband John Payne in Sentimental Journey *(opposite, above).*

Maureen O'Hara – in the best of health (opposite, below).

The beautiful Valli conducted her love affair with Joseph Cotten from a wheelchair in Walk Softly, Stranger *(above).*

Dreaming, alas, doesn't prevent her inevitable demise. She and the little girl are alone together when it comes and she gasps: 'I may have to go away. But it's not really going away as long as we're in each other's hearts.'

To Bill, who is playing a record of the title song when she pays him the first of her return visits as a spirit: 'Bill, dear, my dearest one, this is our song. It will always be our song, as everything we shared together will always be ours.'

The tone of the movie's (Julie's) voice is unvarying, almost hypnotic; the gush of such lines relentlessly mawkish. Yet it must be to director Walter Lang's credit that he holds the interest and makes the tosh acceptable, and Miss O'Hara's handling of her little speeches is persuasive enough to suggest she was a much more resourceful actress than she was usually credited with being.

Variety warned that *Sentimental Journey* was 'the weeper to end all weepers, the film that may be responsible for the five-cornered handkerchief. The current one doesn't seem

SILENT SUFFERING

Crutches and callipers were Susan Hayward's props for displaying fortitude as the crippled wartime singer Jane Froman in With a Song in My Heart, *with David Wayne (right).*

large enough for the Niagara of tears that must surely flow.'

Such were its financial rewards at the box office that it was remade in 1958 as *The Gift of Love* with Lauren Bacall and Robert Stack.

Tears flowed no less torrentially for *Paid in Full* (1950) with Lizabeth Scott in the same mould as Maureen O'Hara's Julie.

Stricken with remorse at having negligently caused the death of her sister's child, she resolves to bear one herself in the knowledge that giving birth will literally be the death of her and she will be making amends by leaving a baby for her sister to adopt. This was not quite as straightforward a reparation as it sounds. Both women love the same man ... and the sister is married to him.

The same year brought a breakthrough in the way Hollywood dealt with hitherto unmentionable diseases. *No Sad Songs for Me* (1950) was a moderately effective drama, edging toward the maudlin, which attracted media attention out of proportion to its real worth by naming its heroine's complaint — cancer.

It was the first time the word had been spelt out in a movie. Needless to say, the victim showed no outward signs of it. Hollywood and, it assumed, audiences were not quite ready yet for shock treatment.

Margaret Sullavan, who had starred in two of the most memorable weepies of all time, the 1933 *Only Yesterday* and the 1941 *Back Street*, made a comeback after a seventeen-year absence from the screen as a suburban housewife who, learning she has only eight months to live, bravely sets about preparing her family's future without her.

It was the last picture Sullavan made and behind it lay personal tragedy, as her daughter Brooke Hayward was to reveal in her book *Haywire*.

Margaret Sullavan, as captivating a woman as she was an actress, was also neurotic, headstrong and unintentionally destructive as a mother. She had three children whose lives were all but ruined by her demands, unpredictability and ambition to be the perfect mother.

The first three of her four husbands were Henry Fonda, director William Wyler and Leland Hayward, most celebrated of all showbusiness agents, whom Brooke Hayward quotes: 'I have never in my life known such a perverse woman. And you know something about your mother? She was the most enchanting, wonderful, delicious human being in the world.'

Anguish of the soul: Charles Boyer and Marlene Dietrich in The Garden of Allah *(opposite).*

146

This publicity still of Jean Simmons for Home Before Dark *carefully avoided revealing her harrowed appearance in the film (left, above).*

At the same time Sullavan was making *No Sad Songs for Me* she had begun to suffer from deafness and would soon lose her hearing completely. She died in 1960 at the age of 49 from an overdose of barbiturates.

For all that the new dawn of realism in the movies which the 1950s ushered in brought a more open attitude to illness and its ravages, the old tenets still clung fast. It was invariably the leading lady who suffered, but a leading lady must always present a photogenic face to the cameras.

The beautiful Valli spent *Walk Softly, Stranger* (1950) in a wheelchair, the crippled victim of a ski-ing accident who is caught up in a turgid romance with Joseph Cotten's small-

time crook. When love makes him repent his crimes, she promises to be waiting for him at the end of his jail sentence.

Susan Hayward suffered terrible injuries in a wartime plane crash as singer Jane Froman in *With a Song in My Heart* (1952) but apart from a noticeable dearth of make-up on the operating table she remained facially unscathed, the sympathy vote being canvassed by the sight of her struggling to walk in callipers and on crutches.

Jean Simmons gave a powerful performance as a mentally disturbed wife returning prematurely to her family from an asylum in *Home Before Dark* (1958), but the only external concession to her state of mind was a hunted expression in her eyes and an unflattering scraped-back hairstyle.

Spiritual suffering might have provided the most satisfactory compromise between realism and Hollywood's obsession with photogenics. A disfigured soul doesn't show. But it was not a condition greatly favoured after the strange affair of *The Garden of Allah* (1936), in which both leading characters are tormented by spiritual angst.

Robert Hichens's 1904 novel had been a sensation in its day, selling more than a million copies and repeating the success as a play on both sides of the Atlantic. Its potential for filming, however, seemed minimal.

The exotically named Domini Enfilden (Marlene Dietrich) travels deep into the Sahara to seek 'peace', though for no very clear reason. *En route* she encounters Boris Andovsky (Charles Boyer), a mystery man of few words but many searching looks whose soul shines out of his eyes and is obviously a sorely troubled one.

Well it might be, for Boris is a Trappist monk who has renounced his calling, broken his vows and is suffering the perdition of the damned.

This unlikely pair, sensing they are kindred souls, fall in love and marry at a desert outpost. Nothing of significance happens except long dialogues of self-examination and pronouncements on transcending love and fatalism.

The couple's mutual anguish is finally resolved, to the satisfaction of no one, least of all the audience, by their decision that Boris can only find peace with God and himself if they sacrifice their great love and part forever.

The film was one of the first to be shot in the newly perfected Technicolor process and it still looks glorious. So does Dietrich, in a wardrobe of diaphanous gowns and veils designed to float ethereally on the desert breezes. But it is

*Ronald Colman, an amnesia
victim, lost his way along the path
of true love with Greer Garson in
Random Harvest, one of the most
potent tear-jerkers of the Second
World War (opposite).*

the marvellously photographed desert land-scapes (filmed in Arizona), not the sufferings of the lovers, which haunt the spirit, though the *New Yorker* was moved to describe it as 'heavenly romantic kitsch ... panting with eternal love ... the juiciest tale of woe ever.'

Maybe Hollywood had got it right all along, though. We have to reach back to its great age of illusion for the 'long-suffering' subject that is a model of the genre, best-loved and most artificial of them all.

Mere mention of *Random Harvest* (1942) can provoke sighs of reminiscence and fond re-membrances which transcend the ludicrous contrivances of its plot and production.

Set in a never-never England between the two world wars (in one early sequence a train is hauled by a locomotive of obvious American manufacture), it hinges on Ronald Colman's amnesia, the legacy of shell-shock.

He remembers nothing of his past when he is rescued from an asylum on Armistice Night, 1918, by a sympathetic Greer Garson. They marry and settle down in an impossibly idyllic country cottage which has roses round the door and a crudely painted pastoral blackcloth at the rear.

On a business trip to Liverpool he is knocked down in a street accident. Distant memory is promptly restored, the immediate past blotted out.

He returns to his family estates and in the fullness of time becomes a captain of industry, wealthy and influential. We, but not he, recognize his unbelievably elegant and efficient secretary as his long-suffering wife, stoically biding her time until his memory should return.

She has to be the most self-sacrificing, un-complaining heroine in screen history. So dependent on her has he grown that he suggests a marriage of convenience (largely his conveni-ence), thus becoming probably the only man ever to commit bigamy with the same woman. Though she has never ceased to adore him from behind her self-imposed conspiracy of silence, the marriage is stiff and unrewarding. She plans a trip to American and on her way to catch a boat at Plymouth stops off sentiment-ally at the little country inn close to the cottage where they had spent their first honeymoon.

Meanwhile a 'wisp of memory that can't be caught before it fades away', as he once de-scribed his diminished powers of recall, has stirred and miraculously lodged. He pursues her to the inn. She has checked out. Mystically, his footsteps are guided down the lane to the cottage. There she stands, framed by the roses round the door, tears in her eyes ... and, to be honest, in everyone else's, too.

Oscar nominations were heaped on *Random Harvest*: Best Picture, Ronald Colman; Mervyn LeRoy for Best Director; Susan Peters for Best Supporting Actress; screenplay, interior design and music.

It failed to win an award but, more impor-tantly, it triumphed at the box office, holding for many years to come the long-run record for the Radio City Music Hall, New York's largest cinema.

149

A happy moment in the unhappy love affair between Celia Johnson (Laura Jesson) and Trevor Howard (Dr Alec Harvey) in Brief Encounter.

7

Stiff Upper Lips

THE BRITISH DON'T CRY. They tolerate sentiment but deplore sentimentalilty. An excess of emotionalism simply isn't British, much less to be caught responding to it. The lower lip may, in extremes of emotional stress, be seen to tremble but the upper one must remain steadfastly stiff.

Fallow ground, then, for the exploitative ministrations of the women's picture, this island race?

Not at all. British audiences submitted just as readily as their American cousins to the classics, even to many of the not-so-classics, of Hollywood tear-jerking, albeit with a surreptitious sideways glance to make sure nobody was watching.

Moreover — and ironically — there was in those films an element which the British could recognize as being something of themselves; a quirk or characteristic ingrained in the American ethos from colonial times — determination and fortitude in the women; men who were either gentlemen or cads; story-lines which often turned on class distinctions or a compulsion to rise in society; good breeding, good taste and dignity.

It is a curious, and overlooked, factor in the Hollywood genre that, buried deep in the psychology or motivation of many a women's-picture screenplay, there is a quality of 'Britishness'.

And, of course, British actors were premium candidates for their leading men: Ronald Colman, Leslie Howard, Herbert Marshall, Clive Brook, Ian Hunter, Cary Grant, Brian Aherne, Claude Rains, Laurence Olivier . . .

Britain's own film-makers, on the other hand, have always taken a wary stance on emotionalism. It wasn't that they were incapable of it. Once transplanted to Hollywood, the veils of inhibition often seemed to fall, enabling a craftsman like Edmund Goulding to develop into one of the great directors of women's pictures with such examples as three of Bette Davis's classics, *Dark Victory*, *The Old Maid* and *The Great Lie*.

At least one landmark title apiece came from James Whale (the original *Waterloo Bridge*) and Robert Stevenson (the 1941 *Back Street*) and Hitchcock made his Hollywood début unforgettably with *Rebecca*.

But stay-at-home British directors remained diffident about baring their souls and wearing their hearts on their sleeves throughout the 1930s.

It was the Second World War which released their dammed-up emotions, or at least opened a safety valve for them, and nourished an individualistic British variation of the women's picture in response to the facts of wartime life. With their menfolk away on active service, women turned in prodigious numbers to the cinema for solace and escapism. It was no coincidence that the peak year for British films was 1946 when cinema attendances hit the all-time record of 1,635 million.

The British women's picture was not above borrowing from its Hollywood counterpart —

more so as success and confidence in the genre increased — and every sub-division of the emotion picture can be found in a British variation. Yet there were shades of difference, subtly reflecting national prejudices and emotional reservations.

No British actress or heroine ever matched the dynamism, the decisiveness or ruthlessness of a Bette Davis, a Barbara Stanwyck or a Joan Crawford. Margaret Lockwood alone was cast in their mould for a few roles (significantly, the ones for which she is best remembered) but, villainous or implacable as she was capable of being, the effect was always diluted by a statutory plot revelation of remorse or redeeming justification.

Basically the British heroine had to be seen reassuringly as the perennial English Rose, even when circumstance had rubbed some of the bloom off her.

Conversely, the leading man in a women's picture was invariably the stronger character, often to the point of being masterful, even sadistic. There were no weak, female-dominated men in British's women-orientated movies as there frequently were in Hollywood's; passive, perhaps, or restrained, but never ineffectual and always, at the very least, dependable.

Emotions tended to be stirred rather than shaken. It's hardly 'British' to shed tears, but to be moved thoughtfully, reflectively, is an honourable state. So the assault on audience sensitivities tended to be deep-probing but understated, its cumulative effect one that could be contained and controlled.

The characteristic reached its ultimate refinement in *Brief Encounter*, the basis for its reputation not just as one of the greatest of all women's pictures, British or American, but also as a masterpiece of the cinema.

It was a quality which served the British women's picture well in its best models, applying a veneer of inimitable style and distinctiveness. When intuitive British restraint was flung off, as in *Madonna of the Seven Moons*, the result was ludicrous. Hollywood knew better how to deal with flamboyance and make it acceptable. When Britain tried to ape Hollywood, as in *Bedelia*, a tepid, Yorkshire-set *Double Indemnity*, it came badly unstuck.

> I've fallen in love. I'm an ordinary woman. I didn't think such violent things could happen to ordinary people.

With these troubled spoken thoughts, Laura, the humdrum small-town housewife of *Brief Encounter* (1945), touches the heart of emotionalism as the British perceive it. The very ordinariness of its characters and situation, the delicacy and tact with which they are observed, are what make it such an extraordinary film.

Laura, comfortably and contentedly married with two growing children, is treated by Alec, a country doctor, when she gets a piece of grit in her eye as she waits for the train home after a day's shopping in town.

A chance meeting the following Thursday, Laura's shopping day, leads to lunch and an innocuous date for the week after. So they drift unwittingly and inevitably into an affair they are powerless to control.

Their shared moments week by week are snatched and furtive, but not without a comic element. At the cinema one afternoon the trailer they see is for a torrid forthcoming attraction called *Flames of Passion*!

After each meeting they must take a train back to their ordinary lives. It is this train motif, symbolic of parting and reunion, which gives the story its pacing and continuity, paralleled by the emotive background music of Rachmaninov's Piano Concerto No. 2.

The affair is, of course, doomed from the start. It's not in the character of such decent people to give way to 'such violent things'. It wouldn't be 'British'.

When Alec is offered a post in South Africa they decide together that he must take it and Laura, as usual, catches the train home, accepting her sacrifice not nobly but with stifling sorrow, to make the best of taking up the threads of her ordinary life as though nothing had happened.

Beautifully scripted by Noël Coward from his one-act play *Still Life* and directed with a perfection of rhythm and insight by David Lean, *Brief Encounter* transcends time and changing values through its honesty, tenderness and humanity. The gentle, understated naturalness of Celia Johnson and Trevor Howard gives the story its heartaching elegiac quality.

Both Celia Johnson and David Lean were nominated for Academy Awards.

A handful of women's pictures had issued from British studios during the 'thirties. Two early minor specimens were the work of the prolific director Maurice Elvey, who came closer than any other to ranking as a 'women's' director with his sensitivity for handling feminine subjects (though not strictly women's pictures) like *The Lamp Still Burns* and *The Gentle Sex*.

The themes of *Frail Women* (1932) and *The Marriage Bond* (1932) were carbon-copy Hollywood. In *Frail Women*, a World War I weepie, the silent screen matinée idol Owen Nares played an army officer who marries his wartime mistress to give their child a name.

The girl was played by Mary Newcombe, whose brief career as a romantic leading lady quickly evaporated, but not before she had discharged another Hollywood stereotype role in *The Marriage Bond* as a devoted mother who walks out on her drunkard husband to protect their children but is reconciled with him when he remorsefully clambers on the wagon.

The first talkie of consequence and destined for box-office success was *The Constant Nymph* (1933).

Margaret Kennedy's best-seller and subsequent stage version had already been filmed as a British silent in 1927 with actor-playwright-composer Ivor Novello as the soulful composer Lewis Dodd.

Now Brian Aherne, already a popular romantic lead player from the silent days, assumed the role. Hollywood took notice. Two years previously he had played the poet Robert Browning in the Broadway production of *The Barretts of Wimpole Street*, but it was *The Constant Nymph* which clinched Hollywood's interest in him.

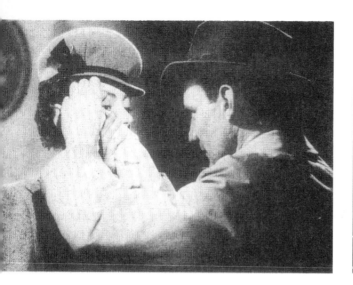

Brief Encounter: the course of a romance that can never be. It starts innocently with a piece of grit in the eye (pic.1) . . . leading to a casual lunch together a week later (pic.2). Mounting guilt is intensified when a friend blunders into one of the lovers' secret assignations (pic.3). The lonely despair of a woman whose love is in conflict with her loyalties (pic.4). The end of the affair (pic.5, below). 'You've been a long way away,' says Laura's husband, gently. 'Thank you for coming back to me' (pic.6, opposite).

As soon as production was completed he was America-bound to make his début — the envy of many an established likely contender — opposite Marlene Dietrich in *Song of Songs*.

It was a neat coincidence that he should be married to Joan Fontaine when, ten years later, she landed her Oscar-nominated role as Tessa in Hollywood's remake of *The Constant Nymph*.

Another Margaret Kennedy stage success *Escape Me Never* (1935) could claim to be Britain's first notable foray into the defined territory of the women's picture.

Its star was the enchanting Austrian stage actress Elisabeth Bergner, who had fled the Nazis in 1933 and was once described by Alexander Woollcott as 'probably the ablest actress living today'. The director was her husband Paul Czinner.

Bergner's performance brought her an Oscar nomination, the first for an actress in a British production, in the year Bette Davis was honoured for *Dangerous*.

She seemed set fair to reign as the queen of Britain's emotion pictures — two more were to follow — but with the outbreak of war in 1939 she concentrated her talents on the London and Broadway stage and never made another movie.

Two years after *Escape Me Never* she appeared in one that is now totally forgotten. Despite its pulp-fiction title *Dreaming Lips* (1937), co-scripted by Margaret Kennedy (sharing an aristocratic credit with Lady Cynthia

Asquith, daughter-in-law of Britain's First World War Prime Minister), found a champion in no less discerning a critic than Graham Greene.

Bergner had already filmed the original Henri Bernstein play in Germany as *Der Traumende Mund (The Dreaming Mouth!)*. Now she duplicated it almost word for translated word in English.

Again directed by her husband, she suffered anguishes of heart and soul as the wife of a young orchestral conductor who errs into a

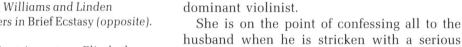

A forgotten minor masterpiece: Hugh Williams and Linden Travers in Brief Ecstasy (opposite).

The Austrian actress Elisabeth Bergner added lustre, for a while, to the British emotion picture (below).

conscience-stricken affair with a famous, more dominant violinist.

She is on the point of confessing all to the husband when he is stricken with a serious illness, from which she selflessly nurses him back to health while simultaneously nursing her secret passion. She resolves the emotional impasse by committing suicide. American audiences complained that the situation was offensive! Graham Greene wrote:

> It doesn't need a critic's praise, although one critic has been so moved by its discreet sentimentality that she has bared her heart embarrassingly to her large newspaper public.
>
> The theatre is packed with just such ecstatic women who squeal with admiration as Miss Bergner's mechanical sure-fire performance proceeds; the bemused and avaricious eyes, the swinging arms, prehensile cooing lips; an elfin charm maybe, but how self-conscious an elf.
>
> And how the handkerchiefs flutter at the close when the policeman reads aloud the last letter of the drowned wife unable to choose between the lover-genius and the boy-husband. The story, of course, is neat and plausible, the acting refined, the photography expensive; it is a shapely piece of sentiment.

The boy-husband was played by Romney Brent, one of the more exotic figures of British films in the 1930s. Born Romulo Larralda, the son of a Mexican diplomat, he was also a writer who, four years earlier, had collaborated with

Cole Porter on the musical *Nymph Errant*, written for Gertrude Lawrence.

He left Britain soon after the outbreak of the Second World War and headed for Hollywood, where he made a modest career in supporting roles including one with Errol Flynn in *The Adventures of Don Juan*.

Better Hollywood fortune awaited Raymond Massey, who played the lover-genius. Shortly after *Dreaming Lips* he too went West and never looked back.

Graham Greene seemed to have harboured tolerant feelings for the British emotion pictures of that year.

Not even another trite title, *Brief Ecstasy* (1937), clouded his appreciation of a film, fairly obscure even in its day, which has lain forgotten for the past fifty years. He has since been proved right, though. With its chance rediscovery and limited art-house screenings in recent years, it has been hailed by a new generation of critics as a small masterpiece.

Its 'smallness' is its virtue. It was one — and the best — of eight productions by an independent company, Phoenix Films, whose short-lived policy before it collapsed was to make high-quality B-pictures.

In the case of *Brief Ecstasy* it is the production values — direction, camerawork, economic but cogent scripting — which raise it well above the average even while its plot hovers persistently round the mean average.

Hugh Williams, later to become a successful playwright, is a handsome charmer who seduces innocent young Linden Travers, a university student, on the eve of his departure for India.

Separation makes him realize he truly loves her but four years pass before their paths cross again and in the meantime she has married a professor much older than herself (Paul Lukas) and is contentedly if unexcitingly settled in domestic routine.

Reunion ignites old feelings, sincere love on his part but more of guilt-ridden lust on hers. A malevolent housekeeper who is secretly in love with the professor — the one false note in the screenplay — alerts him to the situation. His wife has resisted temptation, though tormented by her unsought passion, and when the would-be lover walks out of her life a second time the couple take up the threads of their marriage again, realizing it is all the stronger for having been tested.

This ending, as well as the title adjective, foreshadowed the emotional aura of *Brief Encounter* eight years in the future.

'We can feel proud of *Brief Ecstasy*,' Graham Greene wrote. 'The subject is sexual passion, a rarer subject than you would think on the screen and the treatment is adult.' He added:

> Its French director, Edmond Grenville, knows that the story doesn't matter; it's the atmosphere which counts and the atmosphere — of starved sexuality — is wantonly and vividly conveyed . . . Miss Linden Travers sprawling across the bed behind her locked door, sobbing with passion while the man she wants hammers to come in, represents any human being under the ugly drive of undifferentiated desire.

The disparity in age between husband and wife — Paul Lukas was 26 years older than Linden Travers — anticipated a trend which the coming war and active service for so many of the younger male stars would impose on emotion-picture screen-writers. It occurred again in another small-scale but effective tear-jerker released as war was declared and accordingly overlooked by a public distracted by the turmoil of world events.

In *Return to Yesterday* (1939) British actor Clive Brook, a Hollywood prototype of the 'English gentleman' romantic lead in women's pictures throughout the 'thirties, came home to portray — a Hollywood star returning to the scenes of his English youth.

He and a young actress fall in love. But sensing she will find greater happiness with the man of her own generation whom she has thrown over for him, he deliberately lets her believe their affair is no more than a passing dalliance on his part and, sacrificing his own chance of happiness, goes back to Hollywood and his empty life there as a star.

The film is slight but the tenderness of the spring and autumn romance between Brook and the delightful Anna Lee, 27 years his junior, was delicately etched by Robert Stevenson, Miss Lee's real-life husband, in his last British production before the couple was lured to Hollywood, he to direct a long series of successes including the 1941 *Back Street*, *Jane Eyre* and *Mary Poppins*, she to make intermittent appearances, never quite a star, in such films as *How Green Was My Valley*, *Whatever Happened to Baby Jane?* and *The Sound of Music*.

The most commercially successful British women's picture of the 1930s caught the public's attention just before the declaration of war.

A *Stolen Life* (1939) was also the climax of Elisabeth Bergner's brief career in English-language movies. The dual role of twin sisters, one wholesome, the other flawed, gave dazzling scope for dramatic virtuosity which she encompassed to striking effect. The film was remade in Hollywood with Bette Davis seven years later (see Chapter 1).

As the first crisis months of the war ushered in the 1940s, morale-boosting and encouraging the fighting spirit became the priority consideration for Britain's film industry. This was not a time for sentiment or romanticism.

It quickly became apparent, however, that the cinema would be an important factor in keeping spirits high on the home front. Despite the Blitz, people's demand for movies increased and so did admissions. The British studios began to trim production to the shifts of emphasis in taste. More and more it was women who shaped them.

Dangerous Moonlight (1941; US title *Suicide Squadron*) blended the prevailing war mood with the romantic flavours that pleased them in its novelettish story of a Polish fighter pilot, in civilian life a composer-pianist (Anton Walbrook) who escapes to London and falls in love with an American newspaperwoman (Sally Gray).

They marry and after a snatched honeymoon he flies off to fight the Battle of Britain. In off-duty moments he is composing a piano concerto symbolic of his native land while Hitler's bombs crash on London and the room is crumbling under the blast even as he plays.

The music, by Richard Addinsell, turned out to be an otherwise conventional film's master-stroke. Untitled at the time of release, it came to be known as the 'Warsaw Concerto' and swept Britain and America, probably the most popular piece of pseudo-serious film music ever written.

Its success signalled a mini-cycle of British emotion pictures featuring purpose-composed quasi-concertos.

Three years later Margaret Lockwood was beavering away on the 'Cornish Rhapsody', inspired by the pounding Atlantic waves and seagull cries which provided a high-romance motif for *Love Story* (1944; US title *A Lady Surrenders*).

This one contrived to fuse three of the salient women's-picture themes — war, music and incurable illness — into a cataract of tears.

Miss Lockwood, by now Britain's favourite screen actress, is a concert pianist rejected for active war service when her medical examination reveals heart disease. Understandably stricken by the news that she has only a few months to live, she heads for the Cornish cliffs to contemplate what little future lies ahead of her and encounters Stewart Granger, an RAF pilot who is going blind.

Against her better judgement, they fall in love. But he has already been taken into care by Patricia Roc, a childhood friend who has always loved him and now sees her chance to grab him for keeps.

Craftily, she has made him promise not to undergo the risky operation that could save his sight, thinking to secure his dependence on her. Lockwood counteracts by promising the jealous Roc she will leave the field clear to her provided he *does* have the surgery.

She undertakes a punishing concert tour for the troops in North Africa to keep her side of the bargain. Hurt by her apparent desertion, Granger proposes to Roc, has the operation and happens to be in London when Lockwood is billed to perform her new concerto at the Royal Albert Hall.

The work, into which she has poured her innermost feelings, is a triumph but, for the composer, denied the love that was its inspiration, an empty one.

She leaves the platform to tumultuous applause. And there, waiting in the wings . . .

Love Story was, it goes without saying, an immense hit, one of the biggest any British movie had during the war years. It even reaped some critical approval.

Margaret Lockwood was Britain's favourite screen actress during the 'forties (opposite). As a concert pianist with only a few months to live, she came between Stewart Granger and Patricia Roc in Love Story, *one of the most popular British films of the war years (above).*

Patricia Roc was the perennial 'nice girl' of the 'forties.

'Attractive and even touching at times,' conceded the London *Daily Mail*, while the *New York Times* talked of 'competent, restrained performances by the three principals'.

By now British producers were clamouring for composers who could deliver a pastiche of concert-hall music which would catch the public's fancy.

The 'concerto' in *While I Live* (1946) was called 'The Dream of Olwen' and served the success of an otherwise undistinguished movie so profitably that for a reissue four years later the film's title was changed to the music's.

A baroque melodrama with vague hints of *Rebecca* (the Cornish cliffs again), it had the distinguished stage actress Sonia Dresdel in one of her few screen appearances playing a Mrs Danvers-like personality who, 25 years before, had driven her composer sister so hard that the poor girl had sleepwalked to her death over the neighbourhood cliff.

Enter a young pianist (Carol Raye), fortuitously suffering from amnesia, whom the obsessive Miss Dresdel, a firm believer in reincarnation, mistakes for the sister returned from the dead.

Such was the impact of these three rhapsodic piano pieces, the 'Warsaw Concerto', the 'Cornish Rhapsody' and 'The Dream of Olwen', that time and nostalgia have forged them into a triptych of memories, virtually inseparable as evocations of the halcyon years of the British cinema when people sought just such escapism from the shadows of war.

One invariably succeeds another on recordings and if there is any room to spare it is more than likely to be taken up by 'The Legend of the Glass Mountain'.

Actor Michael Denison first attracted the public's notice as the composer returning to the scene of his wartime service in the Italian Dolomites in The Glass Mountain.

No piano this time. The music forms the basis of an opera composed by the hero of *The Glass Mountain* (1949) who, after the war, returns to the Italian Dolomites to seek the girl who had saved his life.

Theirs is to be a doomed affair — he is already married — but they snatch brief, forbidden rapture before destiny prises them apart and his opera has a triumphant première at Venice's La Fenice Opera House.

Michael Denison, Dulcie Gray (his real-life wife) and Valentina Cortese agonized round the sides of this triangle but, apart from the musical score, the movie's most notable distinction was the first and only screen-acting appearance by the great operatic baritone Tito Gobbi before he became an international name.

It was the war, and the insatiable public need for escapism which nurtured Britain's own individual contribution to the women's pic-

Female hearts throbbed to the suave menace of James Mason (above, left) and the dashing looks of Stewart Granger (above, right).

ture; the costume melodrama sometimes known, after the production company responsible for it, as Gainsborough Gothic.

The forerunner of today's fiction 'bodice-rippers', these tapped a hugely popular if not entirely decorous demand for lurid romance and vicarious sadism in their audiences.

Though hardly 'emotion pictures', such films as *The Man in Grey*, *Fanny by Gaslight*, *Caravan*, *The Wicked Lady* and *Jassy*, with their undertow of unmentionable passions and vices, germinated idioms and characteristics, distinctively British, which would spill over into more orthodox emotional subjects.

And they created a unique star, Britain's first after the war to gain international status, in James Mason.

Few actors have exerted such a disturbing alchemy over their female admirers — a thrall incomprehensible to men. He epitomized cruelty, caddishness and, often, a fascinating corruption in his 'Gothic' roles, and at the first sight of his glowering looks or the sound of his sardonic voice women, if they are to be believed, would feel faint with pleasure.

From the moment he horse-whipped Margaret Lockwood in *The Man in Grey*, British womanhood thrilled, at a safe remove, to the violence he inflicted on them.

In the most memorable scene of many in *The Seventh Veil* (1945) he raises his cane in a fury of jealousy and lashes the precious hands of Ann Todd as she plays Beethoven's 'Pathétique' Sonata (slow movement).

It was Mason's quintessential act of cruelty, calculated to make his adoring fans gasp with

The Seventh Veil, *phenomenally successful on both sides of the Atlantic, brought international stardom for Ann Todd (opposite) as a suicidal concert pianist in the professional care of psychiatrist Herbert Lom (left).*

both shock and furtive pleasure, for behind it, as they well knew, lay the hint that he had inadmissibly fallen in love with his victim. 'If you won't play for me, you won't play for anyone else,' he rages, exposing the depth of his possessiveness.

'The first time I met James Mason,' Miss Todd was to write in her autobiography *The Eighth Veil,* 'was on the set before rehearsal. I was rather frightened of him, but fascinated . . . We then started rehearsing the scene at the piano where he hit my hands.'

The Seventh Veil is among that elite of movies which never seems to pall, however many times it is viewed.

Its origin was a short documentary film the producer Sydney Box had been asked to make about the treatment of shell-shocked soldiers. Hypnosis therapy and truth drugs were among the methods being used and his director/writer wife Muriel Box had the idea of incorporating them into a fictional drama. It was a timely subject. Hollywood was already preoccupied with psychological issues.

In her draft script the heroine was to be a violinist but since a movie about Paganini (*The Magic Bow*) was in preparation she changed the instrument to the piano.

The story is told in flashback, following the attempted suicide of Francesca (Todd), a famous concert pianist. Under hypnosis a psychiatrist (Herbert Lom), gradually strips away the psychological 'veils' of her subconscious to recall her life from schooldays under the domination of her unwilling guardian Nicholas (Mason).

Svengali-like, he has driven her relentlessly in his ambition to make her a great pianist against her will and her subconscious gesture of rebellion has been a series of disastrous romances, each of which he has suppressed.

Of course, the audience — or at least the female part of it — realizes intuitively that the only man she loves, though she doesn't realize it herself, is cruel, indifferent Nicholas.

The film expertly plays on this theme, bringing it to a conventionally romantic conclusion while teasing the audience with a final stroke of the unexpected.

The Seventh Veil was no less a hit in the United States than in Britain and it brought Sydney and Muriel Box the 1946 Academy

Phyllis Calvert, Margaret Lockwood's closest rival in wartime popularity polls, attempted to break out of her 'English rose' image as the passionate Rosanna in Madonna of the Seven Moons.

Award for Best Original Screenplay against competition from such titans as Raymond Chandler for *The Blue Dahlia* and Ben Hecht for Hitchcock's *Notorious*.

In that same vintage year Mason was beastly to Dulcie Gray in *They Were Sisters* (1945), an intelligently scripted but, in its day, under-estimated study of marriage.

Phyllis Calvert is the lynch-pin of the plot, as she is of the three sisters; the only one with a stable marriage, though it has not, to her sorrow, been blessed with children.

Concerned for her dowdy, cowed sister (Dulcie Gray), married to the sadistic Mason, she secretly arranges for her to be seen by a psychiatrist, but when the husband discovers the plan his cruelty drives his wife to her death.

Calvert's evidence at the inquest damns him and she is granted custody of his young children, thereby achieving by tragic default the one element her own marriage lacks for fulfilment.

The *New York Times* opined:

It is Mason's characterization which dominates the varied emotional proceedings. His role is as sympathetic as Himmler's but he carries it off with finesse, understatement and conviction.

Mason himself was not convinced, however. He has written:

We could never understand why the character I played, who in early days had seemed so innocuous, though hearty, turned into a beast in later life. To satisfy me, motivation-wise, I had to tell myself that the sister whom I had married had a heavy hand in the kitchen, provoking antagonism and dyspepsia.

Unconvincing to the point of hilarity was Phyllis Calvert's bid to break out of her English Rose stereotype in the title role of *Madonna of the Seven Moons* (1944), a melodrama which, in its absurdities, reaches back to the origins of the species. Ironically, time has been kind to it. Much scoffed at, it has nevertheless weathered to become a camp classic and, admittedly, is nowadays compulsive entertainment.

Calvert plays Maddalena, the respectable, happily married and deeply religious wife of a wealthy Florence businessman secretly suffering from schizophrenia, the legacy of being raped by a gipsy when she was a convent schoolgirl.

Whenever one of her 'turns' occurs, without warning, she lets down her hair (literally), slips into a seductive off-the-shoulder frock and assumes her other personality as the passionate mistress of Stewart Granger, leader of a gang of underworld crooks. After each of these flings, she returns to the family hearth unaware of what she has been up to!

The situation becomes as wild as the story is wildly improbable when her daughter (Patricia Roc) attempts to discover her secret and is abducted by the rapacious brother of her mother's lover. Deceit, double-cross and death (Maddalena's) bring the farrago to a tear-drenched close.

With its heady mix of religion and sexuality the overall effect is rollickingly hypnotic, thanks largely to its flamboyant art direction and camerawork.

166

The performances are a different matter. Much of the film's entertainment value, unintended though it may have been, is due to the impeccably stage-trained elocution and refined English vowels of these would-be 'Italians', the Anglo-Saxon fastidiousness of their Latin 'abandon' and, not least, the all-too-obvious fact that 'mother' Calvert was in real life only three years the senior of 'daughter' Roc!

All this time Margaret Lockwood was the reigning queen of the Gainsborough lot and Britain's screen popularity polls.

Far and away the most positive in personality and glamorously sophisticated in style among her peers, she was to immortalize herself as a 'wicked lady', branded with the title and persona of her most successful movie.

In fact, throughout her long career, she por-

168

Margaret Lockwood, married to
French aristocrat Paul Dupuis, had
to cope with blindness and a
murderously jealous rival in
Madness of the Heart (opposite).

trayed only three heroines who were notionally 'wicked', in *The Man in Grey*, *The Wicked Lady* and *Bedelia*.

Outside the costume melodramas she was generally ill-used by her studio, despite her flair for comedy and emotion, obliged contractually to work the studio system treadmill of nondescript parts in humdrum movies until she broke loose to freelance.

Having suffered nobly and self-sacrificingly in *Love Story*, she submitted herself to a similar fate in *Madness of the Heart* (1949), a title that faithfully bespoke its women's-magazine substance. Style, in the event, prevailed over substance, though for some unknown reason the film rarely rates a revival nowadays.

We are once again in vaguely *Rebecca* territory. Miss Lockwood is Lydia, a self-possessed London career-woman who is swept off her feet by French charmer Paul (Paul Dupuis), scion of an aristocratic family. Soon after meeting him she is told she is going blind. Any emotional disturbance will hasten her loss of sight and an operation is, inevitably, too risky.

Paul goes home to France, believing she will marry him. Instead she enters a convent where the medical prognosis is fulfilled in due course. Persuaded, however, that she has no vocation, she returns to the outside world to find the devoted Paul waiting to claim her.

At the family château she meets Verité (Kathleen Byron, memorable as the mad Sister Ruth in *Black Narcissus*). 'Don't let Verité's soft voice fool you,' Paul advises Lydia cheerily. 'She is a young woman of infinite strength of mind who inevitably gets what she wants.'

What she most wants, of course, is Paul, who has dashed her hopes of marrying him by bringing home an interloper bride. And she is prepared to murder if she can't get him any other way . . .

Novelettish as it is, *Madness of the Heart* makes wily play with filmgoers' emotions and it was a hit with its target audience.

It also signified, with its elegance of settings and wardrobe, the emergence of British contemporary movies from the dour, ration-book climate which reflected post-war austerity.

The trend had been initiated a year before by Anna Neagle, who was to supplant Margaret Lockwood in British filmgoers' affections, with *Spring in Park Lane*, the first in a sequence of light-hearted, well-dressed romantic comedies in which she was partnered by Michael Wilding.

They had originally teamed up for *Piccadilly Incident* (1946), one of the surprisingly few British movies which touched on the emotional backwash of the Second World War.

It borrowed a favourite Hollywood device — the husband, believed dead on active service, who returns home to find his wife has remarried — and reversed it.

Anna Neagle and Michael Wilding, both in uniform, have, for those times, the statutory chance meeting in the blackout during an air-raid, a whirlwind courtship and a hasty marriage before she is posted overseas.

When her ship is torpedoed, she is one of a handful of survivors, together with an erstwhile suitor she had once rejected, who are washed up on a desert island.

169

Three years pass before they are rescued and she turns up unannounced on her own doorstep to be greeted by wife No. 2, understandably disconcerted as a new-born baby coos background sound effects.

The insoluble is solved in the time-honoured, tear-stained manner with Miss Neagle expiring from injuries sustained in an air-raid (thus bringing the bitter-sweet story full circle) and bigamist husband Wilding whispering his undying love at the bedside. The audience was left to its own conclusions about how the mother of his child would fare after the funeral. Not that filmgoers cared: their sheer numbers made *Piccadilly Incident* one of the top British money-makers of the 'forties.

The plot contrivances are easy to mock (it is equally easy to forget at this distance that war conditions actually *did* produce just such unlikely coincidences in real life) but as an historical relic the film is an amalgam of the ingredients so popular at that time. Upper-class life-styles, England, home and beauty, the infectious, anything-goes flavour of champagne romance while sirens wailed their warnings of danger and death. *Piccadilly Incident* still looks an assured piece of work.

In another variation on the same theme, *The Years Between* (1947), the third angle of the triangle provided a novel twist in the 'person' of the Mother of Parliaments.

Michael Redgrave, an MP, is missing, believed dead, on a secret mission. His wife, Valerie Hobson, takes over his seat in the House of Commons and is about to terminate her 'widowhood' by marrying a devoted ad-mirer when her husband suddenly re-appears.

Her presumption in usurping his parliamentary seat seems to aggrieve him more than her unseemly haste to replace him maritally, an order of values cynics may regard as typical of an English gentleman's male chauvinism.

The idea, in fact, was a woman's — Daphne du Maurier's, no less, on whose West End play the film was based.

The winning Neagle-Wilding partnership was renewed after *Piccadilly Incident* in *The Courtneys of Curzon Street* (1947; US title *The Courtney Affair*), an unabashed upper-crust soap opera spanning the whole of what then existed of the century and pitched cannily to the socialist ideal of egalitarianism for which Britons had just voted.

A Victorian baronet's son marries a lady's maid and, having grown old happily through the vagaries of the passing decades, they live to see their Second World War grandson following their example and marrying beneath his station, in his case a munitions worker.

Britain was tinkering gingerly with Hollywood-proven women's picture themes and clichés at this period. Apart from the costume melodramas British cinema had not found an individual signature to put on the emotion picture. *Brief Encounter* was in a class apart, a one-off. The industry still wasn't really at ease with strong emotional material.

While, therefore, it paid lip-service to the standard themes Hollywood had refined into a genre, British directors were never bound by genre guidelines.

Mother-love was touched on in *When the*

Anna Neagle's long career, graced
by a damehood, reached its peak
in a gallery of emotional roles
during the late 'forties.

171

British audiences in the years immediately post-war craved romance, and Anna Neagle and Michael Wilding teamed up to provide it in such films as Spring in Park Lane (opposite) and The Courtneys of Curzon Street (below).

Bough Breaks (1947), produced by Betty Box (sister of Sydney Box), the only 'name' woman producer on either side of the Atlantic.

Patricia Roc is a working girl who discovers her husband is a bigamist just after giving birth. She surrenders the baby for adoption by a wealthy couple. Eight years later, married to a suburban grocer, she wants the child back, and after a bitter legal battle regains custody of him.

The boy, pitched suddenly into a lower standard of living, is understandably unhappy at being torn away from the parents he knows and loves. The situation leads to friction between his mother and step-father and finally, in the grand tradition of movie self-sacrifice, she realizes it is cruel to insist on her maternal rights and relinquishes him.

The London *Sunday Dispatch* advised:

> Here is a story that will have many a warm-blooded woman cooing with delight and surreptitiously dabbing her mascara with a flimsy handkerchief, and every man sighing with masculine boredom. It is essentially a women's picture and as coy as they make them.

A token 'strong woman' made an appearance in *The Loves of Joanna Godden* (1947) with a nod, well in advance of its time, in the direction of Women's Lib.

Ann Todd married her director David Lean after completing The Passionate Friends with Trevor Howard, while (opposite) Googie Withers married her co-star John McCallum after The Loves of Joanna Godden.

161(1) -65

Googie Withers was Joanna Godden, an independent woman of 1908 who inherits a sheep farm and shocks the neighbours by deliberately flouting convention to run it herself without the help of a man.

What starts out as a reasonably challenging view of early feminism cops out at the half-way mark by taking commercial refuge in the fundamentals of the orthodox romance.

After a catalogue of farming disasters she decides to bring a man in on her solo act and makes her choice from the three suitors who have spent the film variously trying to distract her from her labours. The one she chooses is John McCallum, and Miss Withers made doubly sure he was Mr Right by marrying him for real as soon as the production was completed.

Everyone concerned in *Beware of Pity* (1946) suffered in silence. Directed by the veteran Maurice Elvey, who had pioneered the British emotion picture of the talkies era back in 1932, this was based on a novel by Stefan Zweig, author of *Letter from an Unknown Woman*, and is similarly set in Imperial Austria.

An army officer (Albert Lieven), calling socially on a local aristocratic family, pays sympathetic attention to their lovely but hopelessly crippled daughter (Lilli Palmer). She misreads his interest for love and he is drawn inextricably into a situation which, however kindly intentioned, he neither sought nor is capable of handling. When the girl realizes she has deceived herself she commits suicide by propelling her wheelchair over a precipice.

The film was ambitiously conceived and handsomely mounted, creating an authentic impression of the Hapsburg empire and its mores. But the screenplay is muted, the treat-

ment too 'literary' and the effect an illustration of the chronic British reserve in confronting emotionalism squarely.

The same sort of inhibition muffled *The Passionate Friends* (1949; US title *One Woman's Story*), handled with infallible British good taste.

Quality oozes from every frame of this bitter-sweet 'adult' romantic drama. Ann Todd, by now an international name following *The Seventh Veil* and her Hollywood début in Hitchcock's *The Paradine Case*, is torn between dull marriage with her elderly husband (Claude Rains) and the rekindling of an old love when a dashing, much younger Trevor Howard re-enters her life.

David Lean directed. The original story was by H.G. Wells. The production values, with locations ranging from London to the Alps, were imposing.

Such determination to be a quality movie puts a brake on its emotional impact. It wasn't the popular success it aimed to be but in recent years, with its emergence from a long period of obscurity, it has been favourably re-assessed.

Less restrained was the romantic interest behind the cameras. It was the first time David Lean and Ann Todd had encountered each other and, in her own words, 'I was literally swept off my feet'. They were married soon after finishing the film (and divorced eight years later).

A bid to repeat the success of Nöel Coward's *Brief Encounter* with *The Astonished Heart* (1949) went disastrously wrong. Adapted from another of Coward's one-act plays, it starred

A failed attempt to repeat the success of Brief Encounter teamed its author Noël Coward and its star Celia Johnson as the estranged husband and wife in The Astonished Heart (opposite).

Hollywood's Myrna Loy crossed the Atlantic to deal with romantic competition from daughter Peggy Cummins in That Dangerous Age, her only British film (below).

Celia Johnson as an advanced-thinking woman who allows her psychiatrist husband to have an extra-marital affair with Margaret Leighton. He is unable to cope with the emotional tangle that results and kills himself.

Michael Redgrave had originally been cast as the husband but after seeing early rushes Coward was unhappy about the screen chemistry between Redgrave and Celia Johnson. It was amicably agreed that he should take over the role himself. Although he claimed to be satisfied with the result, the public thought otherwise and gave the film a berth so wide that it has never recovered from the ostracism and languishes, never revived, in some forgotten vault.

Myrna Loy crossed the Atlantic to deal with daughter problems in her only British movie, *That Dangerous Age* (1949; US title *If This Be Sin*).

She falls in love with the boyfriend (Richard Greene) of her step-daughter (Peggy Cummins) and as if that weren't problem enough for the family her husband (Roger Livesey) is going blind . . . all this amid the scenic beauties of the Isle of Capri. The film sank under the excess weight of so many emotional clichés.

Exotic locations seemed to take precedence over emotional charge in many of these immediately post-war British productions. Cameras, confined for six war years within the frontiers of home, ran wild all over Europe.

STIFF UPPER LIPS

Merle Oberon ornamented the French Riviera — and rarely-used Technicolor — in *Twenty-Four Hours of a Woman's Life* (1952), another Stefan Zweig story.

As was Miss Oberon's wont in glamorous middle age, she falls for a much younger man (Richard Todd) and in the span of 24 hours attempts to cure him of his gambling obsession. Instead she drives him to suicide.

Once again with a Zweig subject much attention was given to capturing the story's ambience and not enough to transmitting the plot. The movie's lack of box-office appeal indicated that glamorous locations and Paris *haute couture*, however effectively Miss Oberon modelled it, weren't adequate recompense for stilted dialogue and static, dispassionate acting.

But when colourful backgrounds were allied to an embarrassment of story-line situations, as in *Pandora and the Flying Dutchman* (1951), the effects could be irresistible.

Lurid, overwrought, pretentious and endearingly silly, this was the brainchild of one of Hollywood's most eccentric, maverick film-makers, Albert Lewis, who produced, directed and wrote the screenplay.

James Mason returned home for the first time since Hollywood had claimed him to play the legendary Dutchman, a sailor condemned to wander the seas for eternity unless the love of a woman prepared to sacrifice herself for him releases his soul from its perdition. To this end he is allowed to put ashore once every few years and assume mortal shape.

Ava Gardner in her first British movie was Pandora Reynolds, a world-weary American girl incapable of loving, who drifts aimlessly with a colony of jet-setters on the coast of Spain.

No man can resist her. One prefers to kill himself rather than suffer her indifference. She agrees to marry a racing driver but her heart isn't in it. A hot-blooded matador pursues her violently.

Then along comes the Dutchman, and for the first time her emotions are stirred.

The bullfighter, realizing Pandora is a lost cause, stabs his rival, leaving him for dead. Being immortal, however, the Dutchman turns up at the bullring the next day, understandably distracting the matador so much that he is gored to death.

The way is now clear for Pandora to make the supreme sacrifice, fulfil her destiny and join her lover in eternity.

The absurdities of *Pandora and the Flying Dutchman* are a throwback to those of *Madonna of the Seven Moons*. But, bedecked with stunning colour photography — Ava Gardner's beauty was never more ravishingly filmed — and a delirious romanticism, it is a glorious nonsense, justly regarded now, like *Madonna*, as a camp classic.

It is ironic that the British stiff upper lip should finally loosen a little and genuine passion should be spent on one of the last movies Britain's studios produced in the dying fall of the women's-picture era.

But, then, the masterhand that shaped it *was* a Hollywood one.

Epilogue

EVERY FEW YEARS newspapers dust off an old headline: 'Romance is Back in the Cinema'.

It hails a retreat from the violence and blood-letting that have dominated the macho-movie 'seventies and 'eighties. It heralds a return to more genteel matters of the heart — or, at any rate, an up-coming movie which, let us hope, may signal one.

Only one film, its lineage reaching back to the ethos and heyday of the women's picture, is needed to send up the clarion call.

Love Story in 1970; *Terms of Endearment* in 1983; *Falling in Love* in 1985: a new era dawns!

It's a false dawn. The momentum has so far never been sustained. The renaissance of the emotion picture as a regenerated genre is but a wishful thought.

Times have changed too radically for the old alchemy, the innocence and simplicities that made the women's picture so all-pleasing and involving, to be recaptured in a more cynical age.

It's not that tastes have basically changed — only their focus of attention. In a different form the emotion picture still thrives on television, as any episode of a soap opera or blockbuster mini-series will testify.

All its traditions are there, more of a cliché than ever: strong women, the anguish of motherhood, the emotional aftermath of wars, mistresses, incurable illnesses, high-life, high fashion and glamorous settings.

Occasionally, however, the cinema itself can't resist looking back with nostalgia to a more romantic age.

Kramer vs Kramer, *The French Lieutenant's Woman*, *Sophie's Choice*, *Falling in Love* and *Out of Africa* have to a greater or lesser degree recapitulated many of the principles and much of the ambience of those old emotion pictures.

It is no coincidence that each of them has borne the potent name of Meryl Streep, the first star since the break-up of the studio system in the 1950s to project the authority and aura of a Davis, a Crawford or a Stanwyck, implying a prescribed quality of story and production value. Her name above the title is seen to be the guarantee of a women's picture for the modern age.

The approach may be more intellectual, more realistic and far removed from the manipulative superficiality of Old Hollywood. But the emotional pulse is there.

Time has lent enchantment to the view of those old movies, the mundane as well as the masterpieces. Many have worn better than their contemporary critics could ever have foreseen. The craft and professionalism invested in them are better appreciated now than they ever were in the days when they were dismissed as so much opium for the masses.

As long as it continues to be revived on television and in art houses and as long as succeeding generations retain the spirit of romance and the vicarious thrill of melodrama, the emotion picture lives on.

$\mathscr{B}ibliography$

Allyson, June (with Frances Spatz Leighton), *June Allyson* (Putnam, New York, 1982)

Anger, Kenneth, *Hollywood Babylon* (Dell, New York, 1981)

Barbour, Alan G., *Humphrey Bogart* (Pyramid, New York, 1973)

Belafonte, Dennis (with Alvin H. Marill): *The Films of Tyrone Power* (Citadel Press, New York, 1979)

Bergan, Ronald, *The United Artists Story* (Octopus Books, London, 1986)

Bergman, Ingrid and Burgess, Alan, *My Story* (Michael Joseph, London, 1980)

Box, Muriel, *Odd Woman Out* (Leslie Frewin, London, 1974)

Brown, Curtis F., *Ingrid Bergman* (Pyramid, New York, 1973)

Castle, Charles, *Joan Crawford: the Raging Star* (New English Library, London, 1977)

Corliss, Richard, *Talking Pictures: Screenwriters in the American Cinema* (Penguin Books, New York, 1975)

Cross, Robin, *The Big Book of British Films* (Charles Herridge, Bideford, 1984)

Davis, Bette, *The Lonely Life* (Macdonald, London, 1962)

Deschner, Donald, *The Films of Cary Grant* (Citadel Press, New York, 1973)

Denison, Michael, *Overture and Beginners* (Victor Gollancz, London, 1973)

Dickens, Homer, *The Films of Marlene Dietrich* (Citadel Press, New York, 1968); *The Films of Ginger Rogers* (Citadel Press, New York, 1975); *The Films of Barbara Stanwyck* (Citadel Press, New York, 1984)

Dioro, Al, *Barbara Stanwyck* (Coward-McCann, New York, 1983)

Dooley, Roger, *From Scarface to Scarlett: American Films in the 1930s* (HBJ, New York, 1979)

Eames, John Douglas, *The MGM Story* (Octopus Books, London, 1975); *The Paramount Story* (Octopus Books, London, 1985)

Edwards, Anne, *Judy Garland* (Constable, London, 1975); *Vivien Leigh* (W.H. Allen, London, 1977)

Essoe, Gabe, *The Films of Clark Gable* (Citadel Press, New York, 1970)

Essoe, Gabe and Lee, Ray, *Gable* (Wolfe, London, 1967)

Everson, William K., *Love in the Films* (Citadel Press, New York, 1979)

Fonda, Henry (as told to Howard Teichman), *Fonda, My Life* (W.H. Allen, London, 1982)

Fontaine, Joan, *No Bed of Roses* (William Morrow, New York, 1978)

Frank, Gerold, *Judy* (W.H. Allen, London, 1975)

Freedland, Michael, *Errol Flynn* (Arthur Barker, London, 1978)

BIBLIOGRAPHY

Granger, Stewart, *Sparks Fly Upwards* (Granada, London, 1981)

Greene, Graham, *The Pleasure Dome* (Secker and Warburg, London, 1972)

Guiles, Fred Lawrence, *Tyrone Power: the Last Idol* (Granada, London, 1980)

Halliwell, Leslie, *Halliwell's Film Guide* (Granada, London)

Hayward, Brooke, *Haywire* (Jonathan Cape, London, 1977)

Henreid, Paul (with Julius Fast), *Ladies' Man* (St Martin's Press, New York, 1984)

Higham, Charles, *Bette* (New English Library, London, 1981); *Marlene* (Hart-Davis, MacGibbon, London, 1978); *Olivia and Joan* (New English Library, London, 1984)

Higham, Charles and Molesey, Roy, *Merle* (New English Library, London, 1983)

Hirsch, Foster, *Elizabeth Taylor* (Galahad Books, New York, 1973)

Hirschhorn, Clive, *The Universal Story* (Octopus Books, London, 1983); *The Warner Bros Story* (Octopus Books, London, 1979)

Huston, John, *An Open Book* (Knopf, New York, 1980)

Jewell, Richard B. and Harbin, Vernon, *The RKO Story* (Octopus Books, London, 1982)

Juneau, James, *Judy Garland* (Pyramid, New York, 1978)

Kael, Pauline, *5001 Nights at the Movies* (Elm Tree Books, London, 1983)

Katz, Ephraim, *The International Film Encyclopaedia* (Macmillan, London, 1979)

Kelley, Kitty, *Elizabeth Taylor: the Last Star* (Michael Joseph, London, 1981)

Kobal, John, *Romance and the Cinema* (Studio Vista, London, 1973)

LaGuardia, Robert and Arceri, Gene, *Red: the Tempestuous Life of Susan Hayward* (Robson Books, London, 1986)

Lambert, Gavin, *On Cukor* (W.H. Allen, London, 1973)

Lavine, W. Robert, *In a Glamorous Fashion* (George Allen and Unwin, London, 1981)

Leamer, Lawrence, *As Time Goes By: the Life of Ingrid Bergman* (Hamish Hamilton, London, 1986)

LeRoy, Mervyn, *Take One* (W.H. Allen, London, 1974)

Linet, Beverly, *Portrait of a Survivor: Susan Hayward* (Atheneum, New York, 1980); *Ladd: the Life of Alan Ladd* (Arbor House, New York, 1979)

McCallum, John, *Life with Googie* (William Heinemann, London, 1979)

Mason, James, *Before I Forget* (Hamish Hamilton, London, 1981)

Morella, Joe and Epstein, Edward, *Judy: the Films and Career of Judy Garland* (Citadel Press, New York, 1969); *Lana* (W.H. Allen, London, 1971)

Moreno, Eduardo, *The Films of Susan Hayward* (Citadel Press, New York, 1979)

Neagle, Anna, *There's Always Tomorrow* (W.H. Allen, London, 1974)

Newquist, Roy, *Conversations with Joan Crawford* (Citadel Press, New York, 1980)

Parish, James Robert, *Hollywood's Great Love Teams* (Rainbow Books, New York, 1974); *The RKO Gals* (Ian Allan, London, 1974)

Parish, James Robert and Stanke, Don E., *The Glamour Girls* (Rainbow Books, New York, 1975)

Parish, James Robert and Bowers, Ronald L., *The MGM Stock Company* (Arlington House, New York, 1973)

Pero, Taylor and Rovin, Jeff, *Always Lana* (Bantam Books, New York, 1982)

Quirk, Lawrence J., *The Films of Joan Crawford* (Citadel Press, New York, 1968); *The Films of Ingrid Bergman* (Citadel Press, New York, 1970); *The Films of Fredric March* (Citadel Press, New York, 1971); *The Films of Robert Taylor* (Citadel Press, New York, 1975)

Reagan, Ronald (with Richard G. Hubler), *My Early Life* (Duell, Sloane and Pearce, New York, 1965)

Ringgold, Gene, *The Films of Bette Davis* (Citadel Press, New York, 1966)

Samuel, Charles, *The King of Hollywood: a Biography of Clark Gable* (W.H. Allen, London, 1962)

Sands, Frederick and Broman, Sven, *The Divine Garbo* (Grosset and Dunlap, New York, 1979)

Scherle, Victor and Levy, William Turner, *The Films of Frank Capra* (Citadel Press, New York, 1977)

Shale, Richard, *Academy Awards* (Frederick Ungar, New York, 1978)

Shipman, David, *The Great Movie Stars: the Golden Years* (Hamlyn, London, 1970); *The International Years* (Angus and Robertson, London, 1972)

Silver, Alain and Ward, Elizabeth (ed.), *Film Noir* (Secker and Warburg, London, 1980)

Smith, Ella, *Starring Miss Barbara Stanwyck* (Crown, New York, 1974)

Stallings, Penny, *Flesh and Fantasy* (Macdonald and Jane, London, 1978)

Steinberg, Cobbett, *Reel Facts* (Vintage Books, New York, 1982)

Stine, Whitney (with Bette Davis), *Mother Goddam* (Hawthorn Books, New York, 1974)

Swanson, Gloria, *Swanson on Swanson* (Michael Joseph, London, 1981)

Swindell, Larry, *Spencer Tracy* (W.H. Allen, London, 1970); *Charles Boyer* (W.H. Allen, London, 1983)

Thomas, Bob, *Joan Crawford* (Simon and Schuster, New York, 1978)

Thomas, Tony, *The Films of Olivia de Havilland* (Citadel Press, New York, 1983)

Tierney, Gene (with Mickey Hertzowitz), *Self Portrait* (Wyden Books, New York, 1979)

Todd, Ann, *The Eighth Veil* (Putnam, New York, 1981)

Tomkies, Mike, *The Robert Mitchum Story* (W.H. Allen, London, 1972)

Tozzi, Romano, *Spencer Tracy* (Galahad Books, New York, 1973)

Turner, Lana, *Lana* (E.P. Dutton, New York, 1982)

Valentino, Lou, *The Films of Lana Turner* (Citadel Press, New York, 1979)

Vermilye, Jerry, *Bette Davis* (Galahad Books, New York, 1973)

Walker, Alexander, *Garbo: a Portrait* (Weidenfeld and Nicolson, London, 1980); *Joan Crawford: the Ultimate Star* (Weidenfeld and Nicolson, London, 1983)

Young, Christopher, *The Films of Hedy Lamarr* (Citadel Press, New York, 1978)

Index

Page numbers in italics refer to illustrations

INDEX